Lake Victoria and Riparian:

Cultural Practices Enhancing the Sustainability of Natural Resources

Dr. Obiero Ong'ang'a
Dr. Charlotte Anyango Ong'ang'a

gianis
Publishers

ISBN 978-1-7387024-1-1

www.osienalafriendsoflakevictoria.net
www.charlotteonganga.com

Editing by Gianis Linguistics

Dedication

To my beloved wife Regina and children,

This book is dedicated to you with all my heart. You are the most important people in my life and your love and support have been my rock through all the ups and downs.

My dearest wife, thank you for being my partner in life and my best friend. Your unwavering love and commitment have been my inspiration and motivation to strive for excellence in all aspects of my life.

To my precious children, you are the light of my life and my reason for being. Watching you grow and flourish has been the greatest joy and privilege of my life.

This book is a testament to the love and gratitude I have for each of you. May it serve as a reminder of how much you mean to me and how proud I am to be your husband and father.

With all my love,

Obiero

Thank you, Dad and Mom for everything that you do. I hope that this book makes you proud and serves as a small token of my love and gratitude for you two.

With all my love and appreciation,
Charlotte

Acknowledgement

I am deeply grateful to the numerous friends, individuals, and institutions in the Lake Victoria Region who have played an invaluable role in the research and production of this book, "The Cultural and Traditional Practices that Enhance Conservation and Management of Natural Resources in the Lake Victoria basin." Their unwavering support and assistance have been indispensable in bringing this project to fruition.

A special thanks goes to OSIENALA (Friend of Lake Victoria) for their incredible generosity in providing a base for preparations, coordination, and facilitation of the study. Their support has been invaluable throughout the entire process. I would also like to express my profound appreciation to the elders whose profound knowledge and ideas have significantly contributed to the content of this book. Their wisdom and insights shone brightly during the workshops conducted as part of this study.

I would like to acknowledge the late Prof. Oyugi Aseto and Prof. H. Othieno for their dedicated involvement as part of the Kenya research team throughout the entire duration of the study. Additionally, I extend my thanks to the lecturers at Maseno University for their valuable guidance and advice.

A special appreciation goes to Henry Wako Muloki Kyabazinga of Busoga and our dedicated field team members, Simon Arwa, Chimbowa Richard from Uganda, and Dr. Musombi from Tanzania. Their unwavering commitment and hard work made the data collection process possible. I am also grateful to several individuals in Tanzania, including Rev. Father Theodore Walter, Rev. F Atjer Deogratias Rweyongeza, Rev. Father Ferdinand Mwalimu, Mr. and Mrs. Charles Kafipa, and Katoto C. of Ukerewe Island, for their invaluable assistance.

I would like to express my heartfelt thanks to Kayis Fulgencio from Uganda and Prof. G.E.M. Ogutu from the University of Nairobi for generously dedicating their time and expertise in reviewing the draft of this document. Their technical inputs have significantly enhanced the quality of the text.

Lastly, I would like to acknowledge the financial support provided by the Regional Land Management Unit RELMA (SIDA). Without their generous funding, this study would not have been possible.

Once again, I extend my deepest appreciation to all those who have contributed to this project. Your unwavering assistance and collaborative spirit have been instrumental, and I am truly grateful for your unwavering commitment to the conservation and management of natural resources in the Lake Victoria basin.

Table of content

LIST OF TABLES

LIST OF PICTURES

ACRONYMS AND ABBREVIATIONS

RELMA   - Regional Land Management
OSIENALA - Friends of Lake Victoria
NGOs   - Non-Governmental Organizations
CBOs   - Community-Based Organization
ICRAFT   - International Centre for Research in Agroforestry

Preface

For many years generations of Lake Victoria communities were known to practice ecological prudence, that is, they were exercising restraint in the use of resources to ensure their availability at a stable or higher level in the long run. Through cultural norms, communities learnt to assume cautious and profligate patterns of resource use. They wisely exploited the resources for their daily needs and moved to other areas whenever the resources were reduced. These kinds of cultural practices helped the resources to regenerate.

However, in contrast, the present practices of resource management are more exploitative than conserving, leading to the depletion of natural resources. The present irreparable loss imprudently is incurred against nature, such as the depletion of the ozone layer, which is the most essential factor in protecting life on earth. Drastic climatic changes, exhaustion of finite natural resources, deforestation, multifaceted environmental and human pollution, etc., are some of the well-known serious factors threatening life on earth. This degradation of resources has occurred because humanity has abandoned cultural practices that helped to determine the wise exploitation of resources. In areas where cultural practices are strictly observed in the management of natural resources, we find abundant resources, e.g., Ramogi and Gwassi Hills in Kenya.

Culture is a pattern of behavior that is learnt from other members of the population through culture transmission (Bonner, 1980). It is evident that the cultural patterns of behavior that cause human groups to act beyond immediate biological needs on survival and reproduction sometimes encourage them to refrain from immediate resource consumption. The argument that today's communities with different social structures might not readily accept to follow the past cultural patterns is futile since man has conditioned himself to cling to culture. But we might not be able to maintain our original culture because of globalization. Humanity will be forced to incorporate contemporary science and blend it with the original culture and come up with a new acceptable culture.

At present, there is hardly any empirical research done specifically about the cultures of Lake Victoria communities and their relationship with nature and its conservation. Much is contained in oral expression among different communities especially among the old who will soon demise. It is very interesting that although there are no concrete books written about the cultural patterns of life in the communities of the Lake basin, the cultures are still very much alive and followed accordingly even by very learned town and rural dwellers. The sages are still more respected in the community than the wealthy and politicians. It is, therefore, important that we should not ignore the rich cultural patens that for many years have characterized the harmonized relationship between nature and man. We should rekindle them for both our contemporary developmental needs and natural resources management.

Relevance of the study

The relevance of this study lies in the understanding and recognition of the significant role that traditional cultural practices play in the conservation and management of natural resources in the Lake Victoria region. Before the influence of Western civilization and colonial rule, African communities had well-established cultural practices that guided their way of life and ensured the sustainable use of resources.

Although Western culture has made its way into African societies, it is evident that African culture has not been completely overshadowed or abandoned. There is a resilience and preservation of cultural norms that continue to shape the behaviors and values of the African population, even among the educated individuals. Furthermore, African culture has shown its compatibility with technological development, indicating that it can coexist and integrate harmoniously with modern advancements.

The timing of this study is particularly crucial due to the ongoing efforts of regional integration within East Africa, exemplified by the establishment of the East African Community. This integration provides an opportunity for the member states to unite and collaborate on issues such as conservation, management, and development of natural resources in the Lake Victoria basin. With a population of over 32 million people residing in the region, the study of cultural practices becomes even more relevant in fostering cooperation and mobilizing communities towards these shared goals.

This book serves as an initial exploration into the role of traditional cultures in the conservation and management of the lake and its resources. It acknowledges that this study is only the beginning of a comprehensive and long-term undertaking. There is an urgent need to document the patterns of cultural norms to harness their potential in mobilizing communities and promoting strong cooperation.

By understanding and appreciating the traditional cultural practices that have been historically intertwined with resource management, policymakers, researchers, and communities can collaborate more effectively in the sustainable utilization of the region's resources. This study sets the foundation for further research and initiatives that will contribute to the long-term conservation and development of the Lake Victoria basin.

Organization of the book

The book is organized as follows: Chapter One serves as an Introduction and Summary, providing a brief overview of the subject. In Chapter Two, the study explores various significant issues, including the cultural significance of Lake Victoria, a historical background of the Lake Victoria basin, the role of culture in natural resource management, indigenous management practices, conservation efforts for animals and biodiversity, and examination of cultural practices. Additionally, the roles of external agencies such as the Japanese Government and the World Bank are examined.

Chapters three to five focus on the roles of traditional kings, women, and youth in the management and preservation of natural resources like land, forests, trees, and medicinal plants within the Lake Victoria basin. These chapters extensively analyze the indispensable contributions made by these individuals in conserving the region's natural resources.

Chapters six and seven delve into the impact of advanced technology on conservation practices. They discuss both traditional and scientific methods applied to natural resources and biodiversity. Particularly intriguing is the contrast between taboos and beliefs in relation to the conservation of fisheries, vegetation, and other natural resources. The focus also extends to the trawling fisheries currently utilized by "outsiders" in Lake Victoria.

Chapter eight explores the rich cultural sites that were utilized to educate the youth in the Lake Victoria region. This chapter provides insights into the moral and respectable lives led by our people, especially the kings. It enables readers to analyze the phenomena of transition, change, and the enduring factors in our lives.

While acknowledging the value of traditional and modern approaches to conserving our cultural heritage and practices, there is a looming danger of precious natural resources, including plants, birds, fishes, and animals, facing the threat of extinction. Chapters 10 and 11 thoroughly examine these risks. Chapter 12 focuses on the role of indigenous languages in the conservation of natural resources within the Lake Victoria Region.

Finally, Chapter 13 concludes the book by presenting recommendations and conclusions on how to effectively conserve our natural heritage.

Abstract

This study investigates the cultural practices that contribute to the conservation and management of natural resources in the Lake Victoria region. The research focuses on the Buganda and Busoga Kingdoms in Uganda, the Sukuma, Ukerewe, and Haya peoples of Tanzania, and the Luo, Suba, and Samia peoples in Kenya.

The research methodology involved interviews with community sages and elderly individuals, observation, and workshop discussions. Prior to the field interviews, an extensive literature review was conducted to gather information and identify research gaps.

Lake Victoria is home to approximately 30 million people who have engaged in trade, intermarriage, and peaceful coexistence for centuries. As a result, certain cultural practices have been adopted across the entire region as different ethnic groups exchange customs and traditions. For example, the Baganda, Sukuma, Kerewe, Basoga, and Samia people (in both Uganda and Kenya) all believe in totems. This tradition has helped conserve a variety of animals and trees, as people refrain from killing animals or cutting down certain plants. Strong kingdoms like Buganda or Busoga have enforced conservation through royal decrees, while chiefdoms in the Sukuma and Ukerewe areas have similar traditions, with chiefs intervening to protect the environment.

Cultural leaders have historically declared limited hunting and fishing seasons to regulate these activities and allow animals and fish to reproduce undisturbed. Many forests, wetlands, and beaches were regarded as sacred and served as sanctuaries for animals while protecting the surrounding vegetation. In response to population growth, communities would migrate to more open land, a practice that is no longer feasible due to present land tenure laws in East Africa.

Different communities followed various land tenure systems, such as the Nyarubanja pattern in the Kagera region, the Mailo system practiced by the Baganda, and communal lands administered by elders. These systems facilitated joint efforts to control soil erosion and floods.

The region boasts numerous cultural sites, with Budhaghali rapids on the Nile River, where it leaves Lake Victoria, being particularly notable. Cherished by the Basoga, the site is surrounded by myths and legends, with its waters believed to possess mystical healing powers. The forest in the area remains untouched and sacred, with cutting down any of its trees considered taboo.

Traditional conservation methods included using ash to preserve cereals, utilizing tobacco leaves to eliminate ticks from cows, and treating fungal diseases in crops with hippopotamus dung. Hand-hoes made from homemade iron were used to dig without causing soil erosion, and hunting and fishing tools were designed to minimize destructiveness.

However, the present environmental and resource management systems appear to be less effective than the traditional cultural approach. The negative impact of mismanagement is already evident, with Lake Victoria suffering from pollution and a decline in fish varieties due to poor management practices. Activities like fishing with poison, explosives, or trawlers have been detrimental to the fish stock. Additionally, commercial fishing has encouraged competitive exploitation of the lake. The proliferation of water hyacinth, seen by some as a sanctuary for breeding fish and by others as a hindrance to boat movement and a threat to fishing gear, further complicates the situation.

The study concludes that the destruction of culture as a foundation for environmental management has led to the degradation of resources in the Lake Victoria region. It recommends the revival or strengthening of cultural institutions such as kingdoms and chiefdoms to promote conservation. Communities should be mobilized for intensive afforestation efforts, and fishing on Lake Victoria should be restricted. Community-based organizations (CBOs), non-governmental organizations (NGOs), and government agencies should be sensitized to environmental issues. The study also proposes the establishment of a cultural framework for Lake Victoria.

Chapter 1
Introduction

Objectives of the Study

The objective of this study is to comprehensively discuss and analyze traditional cultural practices that contribute to sustainable environmental management and conservation. The study focuses on the cultural practices of the communities residing in the Lake Victoria region, examining their socio-cultural conservation norms, taboos, and the potential consequences of violating these norms. Furthermore, it explores the role and impact of gender, religion, and Western culture in relation to the conservation of natural resources. The study also delves into the cultural tools and arrangements employed for conserving natural resources, and reviews the historical and present cultural practices, knowledge, and socio-cultural institutions involved in resource conservation. Additionally, it investigates the role and significance of ethnicity, government policies, and institutions in either enhancing or inhibiting cultural practices related to the conservation of natural resources. Ultimately, the study aims to shed light on the evolving role and importance of socio-cultural practices in the conservation of natural resources in a dynamic and ever-changing world.

Specific Objectives

The study aims to achieve the following specific objectives:
* Review past, present, and potential future cultural practices employed by communities within the Lake Victoria Basin for environmental conservation.

- Assess the effectiveness, limitations, and future prospects of these practices in the context of community development and environmental conservation.
- Explore the viability and potential of socio-cultural practices in adapting to a dynamic and technologically advancing world.
- Investigate the influence of gender, religion, ethnicity, government policies, and institutions on the conservation of natural resources in the region and their impact on development efforts.
- Collect and provide valuable data for the proposed cultural dimension of the data bank, which will serve as a crucial resource for researchers, policymakers, community leaders, donor communities, development agencies, and government policymakers.
- Examine the role of indigenous languages in the conservation of natural resources in the Lake Victoria region.
- Revitalize and strengthen the socio-cultural bonds among communities in the Lake Victoria basin within the framework of the revived East African Community, aiming to mobilize them for effective and sustainable environmental conservation.

Methodology of the Study

The following methodology is adopted for the study;
- Deskwork involving the review of literature on the Lake Victoria basin and its people.
- Field visits and personal interviews as well as discussions with the cultural mentors of the various communities in the region in order to acquire data to supplement information from the readings.
- Visiting and listing historical and cultural conservation sites in order to gain additional information through recording for case studies, etc.
- Organization of local and regional cultural workshops and seminars on cultural issues to discuss various cultural issues on the conservations of natural resources and effective management

of the sources of the Lake Victoria region.

Guided by the objectives, the study investigates the traditional cultural practices that have in general promoted the conservation and management of natural resources around Lake Victoria and explores the potential use for the effective and sustainable restoration and management of Lake Victoria Basin and its resources. The study covers the Buganda and Busoga Kingdoms in Uganda, the Sukuma, Ukerewe and the Haya people of Tanzania, and the Luo, Suba, and Samia people in Kenya. These are the major groups living along the shores of Lake Victoria.

About Lake Victoria and Its Environment

A study of Lake Victoria and its basin is exciting and reveals valuable secrets of the people. Lake Victoria is the second largest freshwater lake in the world with a surface area of some 668,000 km2. The lake straddles the Equator at an altitude of 1,135 meters above sea level. It is shared by Kenya (6%), Uganda (45%) and Tanzania (49%). The entire drainage basin covers an area of 258,000km2. The shoreline is irregular and is 3,450 km long, with 17% in Kenya, 33% in Tanzania and 50% in Uganda of the total catchments area of 180,950 km2, Burundi accounts for 7.2% Kenya 21.5%, Rwanda 11.4%, Tanzania 44.0% and Uganda 15.9%.

Major rivers draining into the lake include Kagera, Mara, Mori, Suguti, Grumet, Ngono, Mogongo, Mbalageti in Tanzania; Ruizi, Kibala and Katonga in Uganda; and Kuja, Awach, Sond-Miriu, Nyando, Nzoia, Yala, Soi and Gucha in Kenya.

The lake and the associated rivers contribute significantly to the economic development of the lake basin. The lake provides food and fresh water for both domestic and agricultural purposes. The resources of the lake are also used for industrial inputs and provides opportunities for the development of facilities for transport, recreation, tourism and bio-diversity conservation. The basin is also endowed with favourable climate and rich soil, making agriculture, especially small scale farming the dominant occupation for the people living in the rural areas.

3

The study covers the entire lacustrine region bordering Lake Victoria and a bit of its water catchment area. Although people who inhabit the region are diverse in cultural practices, they have had a common historical background.

They have also had close interaction through fishing and inter-marriage. The people of this region, like others all over the world, have also had to contend with difficult common climatic and weather conditions such as the vagaries of weather, environmental changes and so on. In encountering these conditions, they adopted similar ways as they learned from one another. Nevertheless, each ethnic group has retained its own idiosyncratic cultural ways of managing the environment. This is indeed a remarkable feature of the region.

This study presents an analysis of successes, failures, and opportunities pertaining to socio-cultural practices in the conservation of natural resources. It proposes strategies for reviving and strengthening socio-cultural institutions and practices that hold potential for effective resource conservation. Moreover, the study considers recommendations put forth by community mentors regarding the integration of socio-cultural practices into national natural resource management programs. These perspectives are reflected in the examination of cultural norms, taboos, and practices associated with sustainable development and the conservation of natural resources. Furthermore, the study explores significant cultural sites, such as forests, hills, rivers, wells, bays, and rocks, known for their captivating and awe-inspiring landscapes.

Fisheries Activity around the Lake

Fisheries activity around Lake Victoria is a significant economic sector, with approximately 100,000 people directly employed in the industry and many more benefiting from it. The trade involves various participants, including fishermen who catch the fish, predominantly women involved in selling fish in local market centers, as well as large-scale fish processors and exporters. The annual fish catch from Lake Victoria is estimated to generate around

US $300-400 million. However, the exploitation of fisheries faces challenges due to competition between large-scale processors and small-scale artisanal fishers.

In the context of fish trading, some individuals supply fish to the large-scale factories using trawling as a fishing method. Although trawling has been identified as a contributing factor to overfishing in the lake, it is essential to recognize that fish decline in the lake is influenced by multiple factors. The impact of fishing activities on fish stocks should be examined in conjunction with other significant factors affecting the lake's ecosystem.

Problems Encountered in Lake Victoria and within its Basin

The Lake Victoria region and its basin face several significant problems that have had adverse effects on the environment and the livelihoods of the local communities. One of the primary concerns is land degradation, which poses a threat to food production and the economic well-being of the rapidly growing population in the region. Soil erosion, deforestation, flooding, and overgrazing have led to a decline in soil fertility, making it challenging to sustain agricultural activities. Furthermore, the destruction of wetlands and water pollution from various sources have had a detrimental impact on the fisheries, resulting in reduced fish stocks and overall biodiversity. Fishing practices involving the use of poison, explosives, and trawlers have also contributed to the decline of fish species in the lake. Previously, the lake supported a more diverse range of fish species, but currently, only three dominant species make up the majority of the catch. These unsustainable exploitation approaches highlight the urgent need for better management strategies for the lake's fisheries.

Another significant problem in the region is rampant poverty, which has further exacerbated the deteriorating conditions. Poverty is widespread, and it serves as a key motivation for studying the basin. While the specific pattern of poverty varies in different countries within the basin, the districts in the Lake Basin of Kenya and Tanzania are particularly affected, characterized as "food poor" and "hardcore poverty areas." In Kenya, for example, a 1994 survey revealed that the rural populations in Nyanza, Western, and Rift Valley Provinces, which are part of the Lake Basin, constitute about 50% of the national population and face high levels of food poverty and absolute poverty. Kisumu, the largest city in the Lake Victoria Basin, experiences some of the highest levels of food poverty and absolute poverty among urban areas in Kenya. These poverty levels contribute to the challenges faced in the region and necessitate focused efforts to address socio-economic disparities and improve the well-being of the local communities.

People within Lake Victoria

The Lake Victoria Basin is home to one of the most densely populated and economically challenged rural communities in the world. The current estimates place the population in the region at between 25 to over 30 million people. In 1997, the population was approximately 21 million, with distribution among the three countries as follows: around 11 million in Kenya, 5 million in Tanzania, and 5 million in Uganda. Women make up just over 50% of the population, and the overall population growth rate in the entire Lake Victoria region was estimated to be around 3% per annum in 1997. Notably, the urban population growth rate for towns, municipalities, and cities has been higher at about 7% per annum. The basin has a significant proportion of youth, with more than 50% of the population being young individuals in need of more gainful employment opportunities to mitigate the risks of social insecurity. Addressing the employment needs of the youth is crucial for fostering a more stable and prosperous future for the Lake Victoria region.

Traditional Cultures of the people Around Lake Victoria

The traditional cultures of the people living around Lake Victoria have played a significant role in shaping their relationship with the environment. With a population of approximately

6

30 million, these communities have a long history of trade, intermarriage, and peaceful coexistence. As a result, certain cultural practices have become shared across different ethnic groups, as they adopt customs and traditions from one another. For instance, the Baganda, Sukuma, Kerewe, Basoga, and Samia people all share a belief in totems, which has contributed to the conservation of various animal species and vegetation. The protection of these resources was enforced by traditional authorities, and in regions with strong kingdoms like Buganda or Busoga, the king's edict on conservation was regarded as law. Similarly, the chiefdoms in Sukuma and Ukerewe areas upheld similar traditions, with chiefs or kings intervening to safeguard the environment when necessary.

Cultural leaders in these communities possessed valuable knowledge about the reproductive cycles of animals and fish. They would declare specific periods as hunting or fishing free seasons to protect these species, allowing them to multiply. During these seasons, the people would engage in other traditional activities, such as circumcisions or crop harvesting, ensuring that hunting or fishing did not take place. Additionally, certain forests, wetlands, and beaches held sacred status and were solely used for religious rites. These sacred sites served as safe habitats for animals and also protected the surrounding vegetation.

However, the shift from traditional or tribal land tenure policies to government management has weakened the role of culture in nature conservation. In the past, people freely migrated to open lands as a means to alleviate pressure on specific areas and prevent land degradation. Unfortunately, this migratory practice is no longer possible due to the present land demarcation system in East Africa.

Different communities in the region had diverse land tenure systems. The Kagera region followed the Nyarubanja pattern, the Baganda practiced the Mailo system, and the remaining communities lived on communal lands administered by elders. Through these systems, joint efforts were made to control soil erosion and floods, while also safeguarding cultural sites.

The Lake Victoria region is home to several famous cultural sites, including the Budhaghali rapids on the Nile River in Busoga,

Uganda. This enchanting site holds great significance for the Basoga people, with numerous myths and legends associated with it. The waters of the rapids are believed to possess mystical healing powers, while the surrounding forest has remained untouched over the years due to its use in sacrificial rituals. Cutting down any of the trees within this forest is considered a taboo, emphasizing the cultural reverence and preservation of natural resources.

Overall, the traditional cultures of the people around Lake Victoria have provided a framework for environmental conservation and sustainable practices. However, the changing land tenure policies and other factors have posed challenges to the continuation of these cultural practices, highlighting the importance of revitalizing and preserving these valuable traditions.

Impact of Colonialism on African Cultural Practices

The impact of colonialism on African cultural practices in the Lake Victoria region has been profound. The introduction of new technologies from the West undermined the emerging local practices, including indigenous conservation methods. The arrival of Christianity and Islam brought with them different worldviews, including concepts of creation, nature, and moral values that did not align with the deep spiritual relationship and respect the indigenous people had for the earth.

Studies, such as the one conducted by Bagachwa et al. (1994) in Tanzania, reveal a stark contrast in the perception of natural resource conservation between the local people and the "alien" individuals who gained control over the lands. Traditional land users were deemed incapable of managing their resources, despite their extensive knowledge and successful resource management practices. Pastoralists, for example, possessed valuable environmental knowledge that facilitated sustainable resource regeneration. Unfortunately, this indigenous wisdom was often disregarded in favor of external scientific, political, geographical, and economic approaches to environmental management, which yielded limited success in addressing the environmental crisis.

The introduction of foreign practices and substances further exacerbated the degradation of the region's biodiversity. Chemical pesticides, fertilizers, and uncontrolled discharge of industrial waste, unfamiliar to the indigenous communities, had adverse effects on the environment. The interference with traditional cultural practices disrupted the effective methods of environmental conservation that had been in place.

To reverse the current trend of environmental degradation, it is crucial to take urgent and transformative measures. Cultural institutions such as Kingdoms, Chiefdoms, and Councils of Elders should be empowered to control resource utilization and promote sustainable conservation practices. By revitalizing these cultural institutions within the traditional framework, communities can be mobilized to engage in intensive environmental rehabilitation programs. Additionally, the establishment of a cultural center specifically dedicated to the Lake Victoria region should be considered by the East African Community, providing a platform for preserving and promoting traditional cultural practices.

In conclusion, the interference with traditional cultural practices as a result of colonialism has significantly contributed to the degradation of resources in the Lake Victoria region. To restore and conserve the environment, it is essential to recognize the value of indigenous wisdom, empower cultural institutions, and mobilize communities for sustainable conservation efforts.

Chapter 2

Culture and Traditional African Conservation of Natural Resources

This chapter provides an overview of the key topics examined in the study, highlighting their significance in understanding the Lake Victoria region. It begins by emphasizing the importance of Lake Victoria as a cultural entity and provides a concise historical background of the basin. The central focus then shifts to exploring the role of culture in natural resource management, shedding light on indigenous practices that have historically contributed to the protection and preservation of the region's animals and plant species.

Furthermore, the chapter delves into various relevant aspects of cultural practices, discussing their influence on sustainable development and environmental conservation. It also investigates the roles played by external development agencies in the region and explores how traditional management structures can serve as entry points for effective resource management.

By examining these themes, the study aims to elucidate the intricate relationship between culture and natural resource management in the Lake Victoria region. It recognizes the significance of cultural practices in shaping conservation efforts and offers insights into potential strategies for integrating traditional knowledge with contemporary approaches to achieve sustainable outcomes.

Defining Culture

The concept of culture is multifaceted and encompasses various dimensions. While it may seem deceptively simple, culture is a complex construct that can be defined and understood in different ways. One broad definition of culture, as provided by the World Bank, encompasses shared values, beliefs, knowledge, skills, and practices that shape the behavior of a particular group at a given point in time. Additionally, it includes creative expressions, traditional knowledge, cultural resources, and skills that contribute to social engagement and enterprise development. This encompasses a wide range of aspects such as crafts, design, oral and written history, music, drama, dance, visual arts, celebrations, indigenous knowledge, architectural forms, historic sites, and traditional technologies.

Another definition, as presented by Encyclopedia Britannica, highlights culture as the distinctive behavior exhibited by humans, encompassing language, ideas, beliefs, customs, codes, institutions, techniques, works of art, rituals, ceremonies, and more. Culture has the power to shape human behavior and can influence individuals to adhere to societal norms, exercise self-control, and abide by customary etiquette. It assigns rights and obligations to individuals, fostering a sense of conformity and voluntary compliance with community rules and norms from a young age.

While these definitions of culture share many similarities, there may be minor differences in emphasis or scope. However, overall, they convey the fundamental idea that culture is a comprehensive and all-encompassing concept. With these definitions in mind, it becomes possible to explore the application of culture to various phenomena and analyze its role in shaping societies and individuals.

The Application of Culture to Various Phenomena

The purpose of the following sub-topics is to demonstrate briefly the various uses of culture in different social phenomena including materialistic, ideological and moral values.

Culture and Conservation of Natural Resources

Culture and conservation of natural resources share a profound connection, influencing how we interact with the environment and perceive the value of our natural heritage. It is essential to recognize that conserving natural resources is vital for the preservation of cultures that rely on them.

Indigenous cultures and their traditional knowledge play a pivotal role in sustainable resource management. Their practices often stem from cultural beliefs and values, leading to effective conservation strategies (Berkes, 2012; Gavin et al., 2015). For instance, the incorporation of traditional ecological knowledge has proven successful in conserving forests and fisheries worldwide (Reyes-García et al., 2013; Springer et al., 2018).

Cultural values and attitudes towards nature significantly impact conservation efforts. Environmentalism, spirituality, and a profound respect for nature can serve as motivating factors for individuals and communities engaged in conservation actions (Cox et al., 2012; Stern et al., 2016). Conversely, cultural beliefs prioritizing economic development over conservation may hinder efforts to protect the environment (Sinha & Chatterjee, 2011).

Amaryta Sen (2001) emphasizes the inseparable link between conserving land features and the culture of local communities. Quoting James Wolfensohn, President of the World Bank, Sen asserts:

> "Whether they live on the plains or in valleys, whether they live in slums or in isolated villages, whether they speak Hindi, Swahili, or Uzbek, people have one thing in common: they do not want charity. They want a chance. They do not want solutions imposed from without. They do not want my culture or yours. They want their own. They want a future enriched by the inheritance of their past."

This sentiment underscores the profound impact of culture on every aspect of our lives, including the conservation practices we engage in. Indeed, all conservation efforts among the communities surrounding the lake are expressions of their culture, reflecting their religious practices and beliefs.

Culture and the conservation of natural resources are inextricably linked, with cultural values and traditional knowledge playing crucial roles in shaping effective conservation strategies. Acknowledging and respecting cultural perspectives is essential for achieving successful and sustainable conservation efforts.

Culture and Religion

Culture and religion are deeply intertwined in the diverse communities around Lake Victoria. The region is home to various ethnic groups, including the Luo, Luhya, Kisii, Sukuma, Haya, Baganda, and Basoga, each with their own unique cultures, languages, and beliefs (Hewlett et al., 2016).

Religion holds significant importance in the lives of the people around Lake Victoria. Christianity and Islam are the dominant religions, introduced to the region by European missionaries in the late 19th century and with Islam having a long-standing presence (Hewlett et al., 2016). Traditional African religions are also practiced by some ethnic groups, showcasing the rich diversity of religious beliefs.

Fishing, a major economic activity, is deeply rooted in the cultural and traditional practices of the communities. Knowledge of fishing techniques, passed down through generations, plays a vital role in sustaining this industry and ensuring food security (Mbugua et al., 2019).

The use of traditional medicine is prevalent among the communities around Lake Victoria. Traditional healers, relying on natural herbs and plants, provide healthcare services deeply rooted in cultural and religious practices (Hewlett et al., 2016). The integration of spirituality and traditional healing methods reflects the holistic approach to well-being.

Music and dance are integral parts of the region's cultural expression. Each ethnic group has its distinct music and dance styles, accompanied by traditional instruments such as drums and stringed instruments (Hewlett et al., 2016). These art forms are prominently featured in various cultural celebrations, including weddings, funerals, and religious ceremonies, showcasing the richness of cultural traditions.

Despite increasing external influences, East Africa has managed to preserve its cultural heritage. Ancient rituals and customs continue to be practiced, and important life events such as birth, puberty, marriage, and death are celebrated through traditional ceremonies. Even with modernization, elements like the dowry system persist, adapting to new forms of exchange while maintaining the traditional cultural significance.

Christianity and Islam have gained prominence in East Africa, although there are communities that follow other belief systems. The arrival of Christianity in the 19th century had a significant impact, particularly among inland communities, making it the second most prominent religion in the region. However, the cultural diversity in beliefs and practices is still valued and respected.

Culture and religion are deeply ingrained in the lives of the communities around Lake Victoria. They shape traditions, economic activities, healthcare practices, artistic expressions, and rites of passage. Despite the influence of external forces, the preservation of cultural heritage remains a vital aspect of the region's identity.

Plate 1: Bujagali Falls in Uganda with a special Cultural Significance

Culture and Land Tenure

In the pre-colonial era around Lake Victoria, communal ownership of land was prevalent, where land rights were held collectively by the community or clan. Individuals had user rights within the communal framework, but these rights were subject to cultural restrictions and the larger group's governance. However, with the advent of colonialism and the establishment of centralized governments that extended beyond clan or tribal boundaries, land ownership policies took different forms, deviating from traditional cultural practices.

One notable cultural land tenure system existed among the Buganda people, known as the Mailo system. Under this system, the Kabaka (king) held actual ownership of the land, while granting chiefs the right to use specific portions of land. The allocation and use of land were regulated by the "Mutaka" or land chief, and the land was intended for specific purposes while considering environmental sustainability. Similarly, in Kenya, land tenure was vested in clans, where elders would assign land to individuals as needed. This practice was also observed among communities in Tanzania.

The public tenure of land, as opposed to modern forms of tenure, had a significant impact on conservation efforts. In the past, land resources were managed through public consensus, often led by clan elders or the Kabaka in the case of the Baganda. Customary tenure provided access to land and the lake for specific communities. When elders passed resolutions regarding land use, it carried a moral obligation for everyone to adhere to them.

The transition from communal land tenure to modern land ownership systems has resulted in changes in land management practices and the relationship between culture and land. The shift towards individual ownership and government regulation has altered traditional conservation practices and cultural norms related to land use. Recognizing and understanding the historical and cultural dimensions of land tenure can be crucial in developing sustainable land management strategies that integrate both traditional knowledge and modern approaches.

In summary, the cultural practices of communal land ownership and traditional land tenure systems played a significant role around Lake Victoria. Understanding the historical and cultural context of land tenure is essential for addressing land management issues and finding a balance between cultural preservation and modern land policies.

Regional Considerations

The livelihoods of the communities around Lake Victoria were deeply intertwined with the fishing industry, which had a profound impact on the region's cultural dynamics. This reliance on fishing not only fostered trade and economic activities but also facilitated social interactions and cultural exchanges among different ethnic groups. The lake served as a vital resource that connected communities, leading to intermarriage, trade, and even conflicts over resource control.

The trading networks that emerged around the lake facilitated the exchange of goods and ideas. The barter system was prevalent, and canoes and dhows were used as means of transportation for trading activities. This vibrant trade network contributed to the spread of certain cultural practices across the region, while each ethnic group still maintained its distinct cultural identity to some extent.

As trade and economic activities thrived, market centers and towns began to emerge along the lakeshore. Prominent towns such as Kisumu, Homa Bay, Jinja, Entebbe, Bukoba, Mwanza, and Musoma developed into significant urban centers, with Kisumu and Mwanza growing into large cities. The common thread linking these towns was the presence of the lake. The lake served as a vital resource for the local communities, providing employment opportunities, recreational activities, and a source of water for both livestock and domestic use.

The lake's geographical and economic significance fostered cultural interactions, as people from different ethnic backgrounds came together in these towns and cities. These interactions contributed to a diverse cultural milieu, with the lake acting as a unifying element among the various communities. Additionally, the lake's accessibility and availability of resources played a crucial role in shaping the cultural practices, livelihoods, and social dynamics of the region.

The fishing industry and the presence of Lake Victoria have had profound cultural, economic, and social implications for the communities living around the lake. The lake facilitated trade, cultural exchanges, and the emergence of market centers and towns, which in turn influenced the regional dynamics and cultural diversity. Understanding these regional considerations is vital for comprehending the intricate relationship between culture, livelihoods, and the environment in the Lake Victoria basin.

Culture and Land Use

For effective land management, the people around Lake Victoria implemented various land-use practices specific to different fields and crops. Among the Haya people in Tanzania's Kagera region, they designated the "Kibanja" for permanent crops like coffee and bananas, while the "Kikamba" was used for annual crops such as beans, maize, groundnuts, and other tuber crops. Additionally, the "Rwenya" field served for partial annual crops and grazing land. As museum records indicate, the Baganda practiced shifting cultivation instead of crop rotation. They would cultivate annual crops for approximately three years before abandoning the land for the following eight years. On the other hand, banana gardens were cultivated for at least 50 years (Kasanja, 2015).

Traditionally, the Sukuma people of Tanzania, like their East African neighbors, primarily engaged in cultivation. They adopted biological, cultural, and physical measures to conserve soil and land. These measures included crop rotation, strip cropping, grass strips, trash lines, and wash stops, collectively referred to as the biological method of soil and land conservation. The Sukuma also utilized cultural techniques such as contour farming, early planting, mulching, tie-ridge construction, and the use of compost manure. Their physical methods encompassed the construction of terraces such as ridge terraces, grade terraces, cut-off drains, and artificial waterways. To address water scarcity, they even practiced small-scale water harvesting for growing sugarcane and banana plants in dry areas (Bantje, 1991; RELMA, 1999; Malcom, 1953; Buldelma, 1996).

In the past, even the Luo people of Kenya practiced shifting cultivation when ample land was available. They would simply migrate when the land they inhabited became infertile. This sentiment is captured in G. Ogot's fiction, where the protagonist Ochola states, "I am interested in migrating to Tanganyika one day. The floods wash most of our land away each year, and the yield is not as good as it used to be" (Ogot, 1996). However, with the advent of colonialism, the migration patterns of the Luo were curtailed. The novel reflects the last generation that moved to North Mara in Tanganyika due to their desire to acquire fertile land.

The Basoga people employed charms to enhance their crop yields. They stored palm seeds and cakes of edible groundnuts with seeds during the sowing period. Among the Luo, a poor harvest was often attributed to the evil eye of a witch. To safeguard their farms from the evil eye and pests, farmers would plant certain plants believed to provide protection. Beliefs in medicine and witchcraft also acted as deterrents against thieves. It was considered risky to touch any farm product if the owner had not consumed part of it. The belief was that if the owner had protected the crop using charms, intruders would suffer harm. However, if the owner had already consumed a portion, the charm's power would become ineffective. Therefore, farmers would refrain from consuming their crops to ensure their continued protection (Onyango, 2016).

The Luo people also observed a hierarchical order during cultivation, planting, and harvesting, where sexual intercourse played a significant role. The oldest person in the clan would lead in these activities, and others would follow suit. This order was strictly adhered to, to the point that one would choose to go hungry rather than harvest new crops if their father was absent. According to P. Mboya, this hierarchical order and the involvement of sex served as a means to deter recklessness and effectively manage environmental resources. Bypassing one's senior in the exploitation or harvesting of resources was considered unacceptable. Today, some Christians do not feel bound by these traditions, as they perceive them to be based on superstition. Consequently, the orderly use of materials and adherence to these practices are diminishing (Mboya, 1995)

Understanding the cultural significance of land use is crucial for sustainable land management practices. The historical practices and beliefs of the local communities offer valuable insights that can be integrated with modern knowledge to ensure the preservation of land and resources for future generations.

Culture and Soil Fertility

Almost all the land was virgin and was always fertile. Traditionally among the three East African countries, land was owned communally. This has now been replaced by individual ownership, which has been made possible through the government's policy of demarcation, and willing seller willing buyer system. This has led to fragmentation and overuse of land.

Traditional practices of land use of the communities around the lake enhanced sustainability. Tillage practices such as soil heaping and leveling, increased soil fertility thus higher crop yields. There was no need for fertilizers since these were in plenty in the soil. Heaping of the cleared vegetation and rough digging also added to the soil fertility.

Culture and Conservation of Forests

Forests were culturally conserved due to their significance as sites for worship, rituals, and medicinal resources. In the Kagera region, forests were utilized as venues for traditional worship and were respected as water sources. They served as medicinal repositories, providing barks, leaves, and roots for various healing purposes. For example, in the Kagera region, the "omubirizi" tree was used to treat ailments such as malaria, stomachaches, and skin diseases (Kasanja, 2015).

Similar to the Kagera region, the Sukuma and Baganda people also had shrines located within forests. The Baganda appointed a caretaker known as the "Bujagali" to oversee these sacred sites, which also served as ancestral burial grounds. The Bujagali was believed to possess supernatural powers. Atkins (1999) documented the impact of a hydro-power project on such shrines in Uganda, highlighting the significance of these cultural practices. The Suba people of Rusinga Island in Lake Victoria also had their forested shrines called "Kibaga." These places, located along the lakeshore or atop hills, were dedicated to sacrifices, inhabited by wildlife, and protected rare tree species. Anyone who damaged these sacred sites faced consequences such as childlessness or death, with the remedy being the offering of goats for sacrifice by the elders to "oso pinyi" for land purification (Ogot, 1996).

Similar cultural practices can be found in Bahati District, Tanzania. The residents set aside specific forested areas for spiritual and religious purposes, known as traditional forest reserves. These reserves are protected by the adjacent communities according to their customary laws. Various areas within these reserves serve specific cultural functions, such as spaces for male circumcision, traditional dances, gatherings for elders, natural springs, places for traditional healers, and sites for the traditional education of young women (Kasanja, 2015).

Certain tree species were given special protection and regarded as sacred. For instance, among the Luo people, the "Oremebe" tree was not used for firewood but rather had cultural significance in cursing culprits who refused to repent or for making solemn oaths. The Bukusu people referred to it as "Kimurembe" and used it to make musical resonators for the one-stringed instrument called "shiriri." The tree was also believed to have medicinal properties against mumps. It was believed that burning this tree would attract thunder to strike one's house. Similar beliefs existed among the Abagusi people, who believed that the "Omugumo" tree could not be cut without dire consequences for the person responsible. The Marachi people living near Sio Port on Lake Victoria held the belief that the "Omurumba" tree would cry if cut, and whoever caused this would face death. Additionally, the "Omupocho" tree was believed to house mythical animals in its large stem cavities, and anyone who cut down such a tree would be attacked by resident animals (Onyango, 2016).

Throughout the lake region, these cultural beliefs and practices played a role in protecting forests and other valuable resources. They served as a reminder of the interconnectedness between cultural traditions, environmental conservation, and the importance of maintaining a harmonious relationship with nature.

Plate 2: A conserved forest

Culture and Conservation of Water and Fisheries Resources

The current state of Lake Victoria's water is alarming, as reported by LVEMP (1995), with a rapid deterioration in water quality and ecology over the past two decades. The lake has become a receptacle for domestic and industrial waste discharge, including agricultural runoff and municipal wastewater, which are major contributors to poor water quality (LVEMP, 1995).

Cultural practices surrounding water conservation are reflected in myths and folk tales passed down through generations. Among the Luo people, there are numerous stories that promote the conservation and respect of water resources, such as "Simbi Nyaima" and "Nyamgondho Wuod Ombare" (Ogutu, 1974; Ogot, 1976). One such tale, titled "Othin Othin," emphasizes the importance of preserving water resources. The story narrates a severe drought in which all water sources dried up except for a pond that provided for all the animals in the jungle. However, one animal, Othin Othin (Hare), would arrive early to the pond, pollute the water by dancing, urinating, and defecating in it. The other animals were disturbed by this behavior, leading the king of the jungle to hold a meeting and punish Othin Othin. Such myths, legends, and folk tales served as educational tools to instill a sense of responsibility and self-discipline in children, teaching them not to pollute water sources (Ogutu, 1974; Ogot, 1976).

The myth of Nyamgondho Wuod Ombare aligns with the Sukuma belief in Ngasa, the god of Lake Victoria. In Sukuma culture, not all clansmen were permitted to engage in fishing activities. Only those descending from the Bategi clan, known as the fishing clan, were allowed to fish. This practice ensured the conservation of fish stocks in the lake. Before embarking on a fishing trip, a fisherman would pray to Ngasa for success and safety. Sukuma fishmongers believed that Ngasa was responsible for the abundance of fish in the lake, thus discouraging overfishing. Traditional fishing tools such as migono (nets) and mitego (hooks) were used selectively, targeting mature fish from specific water areas while avoiding fish breeding grounds. Women were culturally prohibited from participating in fishing activities, based on traditional beliefs and customs (ICRAFT, 1991; Sobbo, 2000).

In this region, water sources were considered communal property, with everyone having the right to access water for domestic use and livestock watering. Among the Sukuma, rivers and wells were built and maintained through collective labor. Sisal plants, reeds, and trees were grown around wells and along rivers to combat soil erosion. If a well became dirty, the village youth leader (nsumba ntale) would organize communal labor to clean it (Malcom, n.d.). The Luo of Kenya referred to this practice as Saga, a form of volunteerism in which people pooled their labor to address communal issues. If the environment, such as water sources, became polluted, the community would mobilize through Saga to resolve the problem. Food would be provided by the parents, and girls would cook it. Certain taboos were observed, such as forbidding bathing at drinking water sources and prohibiting women in their menstrual period from approaching drinking water sources. Similarly to the Sukuma of Tanzania, the Rusinga people of Kenya observed specific fishing seasons for different fish species. Their Kibaga, located along the lakeshore, served as breeding habitats for fish (Sobbo, 2000).

Unfortunately, modern fishing practices in Uganda have deviated from traditional methods. The use of gill nets and seines, along with the practice of pounding the water with clubs known as "tycoon" to drive fish into the nets (referred to as "sekeseke"), are non-selective and cause distress to fish. This method exposes species like Tilapia and Haplochromines, which carry their young in their mouths, to danger. Traditional fishing methods did not pose such risks (LVEMP, 1995).

The cultural practices and beliefs surrounding water conservation and fisheries in the region demonstrate the importance of preserving these vital resources. They provide valuable lessons and insights that can inform efforts to address the current challenges faced by Lake Victoria and its water and fisheries resources.

Culture, Conservation and Management of Wildlife

Wildlife held immense value throughout the region, serving not only as a source of food but also for medicinal and entertainment purposes. Certain animal parts, such as skins or feathers, were utilized for decorative purposes. However, hunting was regulated and carried out seasonally to ensure sustainable practices. Many ethnic groups residing around Lake Victoria considered specific animals as sacred, leading to their protection and conservation. For instance, the Marachi community in Port Victoria revered a particular species of antelope as their totem, resulting in the animal being safeguarded in its vicinity. Similarly, the Nyakach people of Kisumu voiced their opposition when a python named Omieri, which they considered sacred, was killed. The existence of diverse animal totems across clans and ethnic groups meant that certain animals were prohibited from being hunted, killed, or consumed.

Consequently, these animals thrived and multiplied without human interference. The deep-rooted belief in totems spanning Uganda, Kenya, and Tanzania played a crucial role in wildlife management practices throughout the region.

Culture and the Perpetuation of Social Values: The case of Praises (Pakruok)

Culture served as a powerful means of conveying challenging and difficult messages to individuals within a specific age group, facilitating their understanding of how to navigate and manage various situations. Songs, proverbs, and "pakruok" (praise names) - a unique tradition of the Luo people - were utilized as mediums to propagate the values of society. This practice involved engaging in music, dancing sessions, and delivering eloquent speeches that praised one's heritage, accomplishments, and family reputation. The speeches were not only a display of oratory skills but also carried valuable messages for the audience. It was a battle of wit, incorporating tongue-twisters and symbolism. Linguistic expertise and artistic finesse were employed, with a primary focus on cultural heritage, sometimes encompassing environmental conservation. The musicians would compose songs that celebrated birds, animals, and significant landmarks such as mountains, rivers, or lakes, acknowledging those who responsibly utilized these resources.

However, it is important to recognize that not all of the traditional cultural practices described above are necessarily desirable in the present context. Some of these practices have become obsolete, outdated, and unsustainable in light of the advancements in science and technology that have permeated the communities of the Lake region. It is crucial to strike a balance between preserving cultural heritage and embracing new knowledge and approaches for the sustainable development of these communities.

Appreciation of Culture of other Countries: The Case of Japanese Culture

Kodansha Internal (1994) presents a fascinating account of

Japanese culture and its deep-rooted appreciation for plants and conservation. In ancient Japan, the early inhabitants devised sacred rituals of exorcism, ablution, and divination, with the hope of averting natural disasters. It was through these mystic-religious practices and their reverence for nature that trees and flowers came to be seen as symbols of the divine. Notably, primordial evergreen trees such as pines (natsu), cedars (sugi), cypresses (hinoki), and camphor trees (kusunoki) were believed to serve as dwelling places (yorishiro) for deities descending from heaven. To welcome these deities on New Year's Day, the Japanese adorned their gates with pine branches (Kadomatsu).

Another cultural tradition involving flowers is the practice of viewing them in a park. Originating from agricultural rites, this activity eventually transformed into a recreational pursuit. Cherry blossoms, known as Sakura, garnered the largest number of admirers. Over time, an annual cherry blossom-viewing party, initially sponsored by the imperial court, became an established custom during the Heian period (794-1185). This tradition subsequently spread among the common people. Apart from cherry blossoms, other flowers like Japanese plums (ume), wisteria (fuji), chrysanthemums (kiku), and lotus (hasu) also became popular subjects of admiration.

In ancient Japan, nature was regarded as divine, with mountains, rivers, stones, and plants believed to possess spirits. Based on this belief, prayers were offered to these natural elements in the quest for salvation. During religious festivals, evergreen trees, marine products, and fresh farm vegetables were presented to the deities instead of animal flesh. As these customs gained significance in Japan, people began to recognize the importance of conserving and restoring their natural environment. They realized the pitfalls of solely embracing Western industrialization values. It is worth noting that similar cultural practices promoting environmental conservation existed in various other countries around the world. Thus, the role of culture in fostering environmental preservation is not unique to the communities around Lake Victoria but extends to different regions worldwide.

Chapter 3

Background to the Main Cultural Issues Addressed

Culture plays a pivotal role in shaping multiple facets of people's lives, including their pre-occupations, social and economic engagements, and their interactions with the natural resources and the environment. The customs, traditions, and belief systems embraced by communities in the Lake Victoria region significantly influence their approach to conservation. By understanding the factors that influence cultural practices and conservation in this region, we can gain insights into the complex interplay between cultural heritage and environmental stewardship. This knowledge lays the foundation for developing strategies that harmoniously integrate cultural values with sustainable resource management, ensuring the preservation of both cultural diversity and the region's ecological integrity.

The Cultural and Economic Importance of Lake Victoria

Lake Victoria, spanning an impressive surface area of 68,000 square kilometers, holds immense cultural and economic significance. As the second largest freshwater lake in the world, it serves as a lifeline for over 30 million people residing in East African countries such as Kenya, Uganda, and Tanzania. The lake's abundant resources, particularly its thriving fish populations, provide sustenance for the local communities, making it a crucial source of food security. Moreover, the fishing industry and its associated activities employ millions of individuals, offering livelihood opportunities and supporting countless families and dependents.

The economic impact of Lake Victoria reaches far beyond the immediate communities it serves. The income generated from fishing activities contributes to the regional economy and has ripple effects across various sectors. It helps to support local businesses, stimulates trade, and fosters economic growth. Additionally, the revenue generated through fishing plays a vital role in generating foreign exchange for governments in the region, bolstering national economies and supporting developmental initiatives.

Recognizing the cultural and economic importance of Lake Victoria underscores the urgent need for its conservation. Preserving the lake as a vital economic resource necessitates an understanding of the cultural heritage of the communities that depend on it. By delving into the rich cultural traditions and practices of the people, valuable insights can be gained on their inherent strengths in conservation. Building upon these indigenous conservation approaches can contribute to the sustainable development of the region's resources, ensuring the well-being of both present and future generations.

The cultural and economic significance of Lake Victoria cannot be overstated. Its resources sustain millions of lives, drive local and regional economies, and hold tremendous potential for sustainable development. By embracing the cultural heritage of the people and harnessing their traditional conservation practices, we can forge a path towards responsible management of this invaluable resource and secure a prosperous future for the communities and ecosystems that rely on Lake Victoria.

The History of the Settlement within the Lake Victoria Basin

The settlement within the Lake Victoria Basin holds a captivating history that spans centuries, shaping the region's cultural mosaic. Historical records indicate that the initial waves of settlement occurred during the 13th and 14th centuries when diverse ethnic groups established their communities around the lake.

One of the most prominent groups in the region is the Luo

people, believed to have migrated along the course of the River Nile from northern Africa. They first settled in present-day Uganda before later migrating to Kenya. Some Luo communities journeyed even further south to Tanganyika, now known as Tanzania, where they settled in the North Mara District, enriching the cultural diversity of the area.

Another significant ethnic group within the Lake Victoria Basin is the Bantu people, whose origins can be traced back to Central Africa. They primarily settled on the Ugandan side of the basin, where their communities evolved into distinct indigenous kingdoms, such as the Baganda, Banyoro, Toro, Ankole, and Basoga. Among these kingdoms, the Baganda emerged as a dominant force, exerting their influence over the others. However, external challenges in the 19th century led to their eventual subjugation.

The Basoga, another influential kingdom, established their domain around Jinja in Uganda and played a vital role in the conservation and management of natural resources in the region.

In southern Tanzania, bordering Lake Victoria, communities like the Wasukuma and Wanyamwezi made their homes, contributing to the region's cultural richness and resource utilization.

Numerous other groups have also thrived within the Lake Victoria Basin, including the Wazanaki, Wajota, and Wakerewe in Tanzania, as well as the Banyala and Basuba, who migrated from Uganda to settle in Kenya and parts of Tanzania. The Samia community in Uganda also continues to maintain a presence in the region.

Despite their diverse origins, these communities were bound together not only by the environmental challenges they faced but also by informal cultural institutions. These institutions played a crucial role in fostering cooperation, shared knowledge, and sustainable resource management practices. Through their cultural bonds and common experiences, these communities have contributed to the conservation and preservation of the Lake Victoria Basin's natural resources for generations.

The rich history of settlement within the Lake Victoria Basin serves as a testament to the resilience and ingenuity of the region's diverse communities, highlighting the importance of their cultural heritage in shaping the sustainable coexistence with the environment.

Plate 3: Culture and Settlement around Lake Victoria

The Informal Institutions in Natural Resources Management

Informal institutions play a vital role in natural resource management within communities around the Lake Victoria Basin. These institutions encompass a set of ethical rules, values, and practices that bind community members together and guide their interactions with the environment. They are deeply rooted in cultural practices and religious beliefs, and their enforcement relies on social pressures and the influence of religious values.

One important aspect of informal institutions is the transmission of ecological knowledge from one generation to the next. Elders or "wise persons" within the community hold a position of authority and their words carry significant weight. They are responsible for passing on traditional ecological knowledge, including sustainable resource management practices, to younger members of the community. The wisdom and guidance of these elders shape the attitudes and behaviors of the younger generation in their interactions with natural resources.

Additionally, the diffusion and sharing of ecological knowledge between neighboring communities contribute to conservation efforts. Communities often exchange information and practices related to resource management, allowing for a broader understanding of local biodiversity and the implementation of effective conservation strategies. This knowledge-sharing fosters cooperation and strengthens conservation efforts across different communities.

Informal institutions have mechanisms in place to ensure their perpetuation and endurance. Violations of informal norms may result in social consequences, such as questioning a person's social status or reputation within the community. Moreover, self-enforcement is often triggered by beliefs in supernatural or religious powers. The fear of divine punishment or spiritual consequences acts as a deterrent to behaviors that may harm the environment or violate established norms.

Cultural practices and religious traditions are deeply intertwined with informal institutions. These practices have evolved over time and have had a long-lasting impact on indigenous management practices. They provide a framework for sustainable resource use, ensuring that natural resources are conserved and protected for future generations.

In summary, informal institutions in natural resource management within the Lake Victoria Basin are rooted in cultural practices, religious beliefs, and ethical rules. They facilitate the transmission of ecological knowledge, foster cooperation between communities, and provide mechanisms for self-enforcement. By incorporating traditional wisdom and practices, these institutions contribute to the conservation and sustainable use of natural resources, promoting the well-being of both the communities and the environment they rely on.

The Indigenous Management Practices

Indigenous management practices within the communities around the Lake Victoria Basin have been shaped by centuries of living in close harmony with their natural surroundings. While the influence of new cultures and technology has introduced changes to traditional practices, many aspects of indigenous resource management have persisted and continue to be relevant today.

To gain a comprehensive understanding of effective resource management, this study looked beyond the local communities and explored cultural practices from other communities both nationally and internationally. By examining the strengths and weaknesses of these practices, valuable insights were gained that could inform conservation efforts within the Lake Victoria Basin.

One notable strength of indigenous management practices is their deep-rooted connection to the land and natural resources. Indigenous communities have developed a profound understanding of their local ecosystems through generations of observation and interaction. They possess intricate knowledge of the behavior of plants, animals, and ecological processes, allowing them to make informed decisions regarding resource use and conservation.

Indigenous practices often emphasize sustainable harvesting techniques and resource rotation to prevent overexploitation. For example, rotational farming systems, such as shifting cultivation or fallowing, have been employed by some communities to allow the land to regenerate and maintain its productivity over time. By giving the land periods of rest, biodiversity can be preserved, soil erosion can be minimized, and ecosystems can remain resilient.

Furthermore, traditional practices often incorporate the concept of communal resource management. Many indigenous communities recognize that resources are shared among community members and have established customary laws and norms to govern their use. These systems promote equitable access to resources and encourage collective responsibility for their sustainable management. Decision-making processes are often participatory, involving community members in discussions and consultations to ensure that diverse perspectives and knowledge are taken into account.

Indigenous knowledge systems are often holistic and integrated, encompassing not only ecological aspects but also cultural and spiritual dimensions. Traditional rituals, ceremonies, and taboos play a significant role in resource management, guiding behaviors and practices that foster respect for nature and promote conservation. Sacred sites and protected areas are often established to safeguard important ecological areas and maintain biodiversity.

Despite the strengths of indigenous management practices, there are also potential weaknesses that need to be acknowledged. The rapid changes in the socio-economic and environmental landscape pose challenges to the continuity of traditional practices. Modernization, urbanization, and globalization can disrupt traditional systems, leading to the erosion of indigenous knowledge and weakening of cultural institutions.

In conclusion, the study recognized the importance of indigenous management practices in the conservation and sustainable use of natural resources within the Lake Victoria Basin. By examining both local and external cultural practices, valuable lessons were learned that can inform efforts to integrate traditional wisdom with modern conservation approaches. Recognizing the strengths of indigenous knowledge systems and addressing the challenges they face can contribute to the preservation of biodiversity, the protection of ecosystems, and the well-being of the communities living in the region.

Culture of Monitoring the State of Resources

The culture of monitoring the state of resources is deeply ingrained in many indigenous communities, and they have developed various practices and rules to ensure the sustainable use of natural resources. These practices reflect a profound understanding of the interconnectedness between humans and their environment, and the need to maintain balance and harmony for the well-being of both.

In the Kikuyu community of Kenya, for example, certain heavily wooded lands were designated as timber reserves for the community. Cutting large trees in these areas required permission from the clan elders, and the cutting of valued trees was strictly prohibited. This practice aimed to protect the forest and ensure that timber resources were managed sustainably, preventing overexploitation and ensuring their availability for future generations.

Similarly, the Barbers of Morocco had a chief who made important decisions regarding common grazing. This included determining the timing and location of movements, as well as regulating access to grazing areas and deferring grazing to allow vegetation to regenerate. By centralizing decision-making authority, the community could effectively monitor and manage grazing resources to prevent overgrazing and maintain the health of the rangelands.

In various communities, certain fishing practices or gear that can deplete fish stocks are banned to protect the aquatic resources. For example, the Vanuatu people in Oceania prohibit drop-line fishing, gill netting, and spearfishing at night, as these methods are considered destructive to fish populations. In the Sakuma lagoon in Ghana, the use of certain nets with mesh sizes below 2.5 cm is also banned to ensure the sustainability of fish populations.

Ethical considerations are often integrated into resource management practices. In Salamanca, Costa Rica, it is considered unacceptable to leave an animal wounded during a hunt. Hunters are expected to kill animals quickly to minimize their suffering. Selling meat from wild animals is also believed to be punished by a higher power, as wild animals are seen as resources meant for sustenance rather than commercial gain.

The management of trees and shrubs is another aspect of resource monitoring that is regulated by formal and informal rules. Among the Pokot and Turkana communities in Kenya, careful selection of trees to cut is practiced. Valuable trees are rarely chopped down, while less useful bushes are cut back to make fences and control bush encroachment on rangelands. The Gabra community in northern Kenya has specific rules regarding the use of live wood for fuel. Live wood is not cut for fuel purposes, but it is utilized for constructing huts and corrals. Different species of wood are designated for specific types of buildings, and collection of wood for houses is restricted to prescribed times of the year to ensure sustainable use.

These examples highlight the cultural practices and rules established by indigenous communities to monitor and manage their resources. By incorporating ethical considerations, communal decision-making, and restrictions on resource use, these practices contribute to the sustainable utilization of natural resources and the preservation of biodiversity. They serve as valuable lessons and inspirations for modern conservation efforts, emphasizing the importance of cultural values and community-based approaches in achieving long-term ecological balance.

The Culture of Protection of Species

The culture of protecting species encompasses various practices that regulate the exploitation of vulnerable stages in their life cycles. In Oceania, for example, fishing during fish-spawning seasons is strictly forbidden in several communities. This tradition shares similarities with the Luo culture, where fishing was prohibited during the corresponding spawning period.

Similarly, in the Jharkhand region of east-central India, certain species are protected during critical life history stages. For instance, fishing in a fish pool with the entire stock or hunting pregnant deer is strictly prohibited. In Kadazan, Malaysia, there are designated periods when fishing in rivers is not allowed, and anyone caught fishing during this time must provide compensation that satisfies both the spiritual world and the community.

Many societies practice limited harvesting by restricting it to certain months, weeks, days, or even years. In the Tikopia district of the Solomon Islands, when trees or crops are not bearing well, the clan chief has the authority to impose a ban on harvesting specific food items or for a certain period. In Ghana, fishing is forbidden on certain days of the week at the Sakumo and Djange lagoons.

In pre-contact Hawaiian culture, strict schedules were observed for planting, fishing, and harvesting. Certain days were prohibited due to the fear of death, and fishing for specific fish species was also restricted to their spawning months. Only specific days of the month were considered suitable for fishing, allowing the resources to reproduce and replenish themselves, ensuring a continuous food supply for the people. In many societies, certain animals and plants are entirely protected. For example, the fig tree in India, which supports a wide range of birds and bats, is traditionally protected for biodiversity conservation.

In the Aru Islands of Indonesia, certain animals are regarded as ancestral and are therefore off-limits for consumption by specific families. The garotong fish, known for its ancestral resemblance, cannot be caught by those families, as it is believed that ignoring this rule would bring death and disease upon them.

Many traditional societies practice integrated farming and cultivation systems. Communities in China, Indonesia, and Hawaii, for instance, incorporate multiple species in their fish-related systems. This approach optimizes the use of available resources since different species have different feeding habits. Fish farmers in the Zhujiang delta in China integrate fish farming with vegetable and sugarcane production, utilizing agricultural waste to feed the fish and fish waste to fertilize the crops. Pastoralists also adopt a similar approach by grazing different species of animals in the same pasture to make efficient use of diverse vegetation.

Rotation of land use is another widely employed practice. Farming land, grazing land, trapping areas, and fishing grounds are rotated to ensure sustainable resource utilization. Land rotation is a well-known principle worldwide, where different pieces of land are periodically fallowed or planted with restorative seeds to maintain soil fertility. Grazing land rotation is practiced in arid or semi-arid parts of Africa. In Samburu, Northern Kenya, grazing areas are reserved for the dry season. The Waswanipi Cree hunters in Canada rotate trapping areas on a 4-year cycle to allow the beaver population to recover. The Chisasibi Cree hunters also adopt a 4 or 5-year cycle for rotating fishing grounds.

Rotation strategies are also used to preserve forage during critical periods. The Zaghawa people of Chad move their sheep and camels to the Sahara in separate parallel paths, leaving a portion of the land ungrazed for their return journey south.

In certain areas, rotation techniques involving deliberate overgrazing are utilized to increase woodland carrying capacity. The Fulani people in northern Sierra Leone practice "shifting pasturage," grazing in one zone for two to three years before moving elsewhere and allowing the first area to rest for 15-20 years.

These cultural practices of rotation, restriction, and integration demonstrate the deep-rooted wisdom and sustainable resource management approaches developed by traditional societies across the globe. By respecting vulnerable life stages, observing specific schedules, and implementing rotational strategies, these cultures have fostered the preservation and replenishment of species and resources for generations.

The Culture of Protection of the Habitant

The culture of protecting habitats is deeply rooted in the tradition of setting aside areas for spiritual and religious purposes. These designated areas play a vital role in the conservation of habitats. For instance, in the Bahati District of Tanzania, there are traditional forest reserves that are safeguarded by the residents of neighboring areas in accordance with their customary laws.

These reserves are classified into different categories based on their specific uses and the intended users. Some areas are dedicated to male rituals such as circumcision and dances, while others are reserved for male elders. Natural springs within the reserves are utilized by traditional medicine men, and there are sites specifically designated for the traditional teaching of young women. If anyone, whether a member of the group or not, cuts a tree within the reserve, they are obligated to pay a fine to the group. Refusal to pay the fine can lead to prayers for bad luck upon the offender's family, and ultimately, the offender may be excommunicated from the village. As a result of these strict regulations, the traditional forest reserves in Bahati District have remained untouched for generations, showcasing the success of this form of resource management.

Access to most sacred forests is restricted to specific activities and members of the community through taboos, codes, and customs. For example, in the Holy Hills of China, gathering, hunting, wood chopping, and cultivation are strictly prohibited. The Dai people believe that engaging in these activities would anger the gods and bring misfortune and disaster to the community.

In certain sacred groves in Southern Ghana, like Nanhini,

farming, hunting, and collecting snails are prohibited, while gathering medicinal plants is allowed. These sacred groves serve as significant sources of traditional medicine and are utilized by healers.

In the Jharkhand region of east-central India, trees such as Sal, Muhuwa, and Bel are considered sacred and are harvested judiciously for specific purposes and during specific seasons. Similarly, in Koniyao, Southern Ghana, several rivers and streams are considered sacred. Each river has a designated sacred day when crossing the river and irrigating fields from it are prohibited.

These cultural practices highlight the deep respect and reverence that communities have for habitats. By imposing restrictions and observing sacred traditions, these cultures contribute to the conservation and sustainable management of natural habitats and their resources.

The Culture of Conserving Seasonal Wetlands during and after Rainy Seasons

The culture of conserving seasonal wetlands during and after rainy seasons has been an integral part of the livelihoods and traditions of many communities, particularly in areas where permanent freshwater is scarce. These wetlands serve as important sources of water, food, and materials for building and weaving, while also providing critical habitats for various aquatic species.

One such example can be found in the Samia district of Western Kenya, where the River Sio empties into Lake Victoria. In the past, the annual flooding of the River Sio brought great joy to the people of Sianja village. The floodwaters would spill into the Sianja swamp, creating favorable conditions for fish to thrive. This natural phenomenon occurred during the months of April and May, marking an eagerly awaited period for the community.

As the floodwaters subsided, both fishermen and non-fishermen from the village would converge on the swamp. This communal effort to harvest the abundant fish became a significant event, interrupting other activities as all attention turned towards the resource-rich wetland. People would simply pick up the fish of their choice, taking advantage of the flood's bounty.

The cultural practice of conserving these seasonal wetlands was ingrained in the community's way of life. They understood the importance of allowing the wetlands to flourish during the rainy season, as it directly impacted their access to vital resources. The annual flooding ensured a sustainable supply of fish, providing food security and economic opportunities for the villagers.

However, over time, several factors have contributed to the reduction of annual flooding on the River Sio and the subsequent impact on the wetland ecosystem. Changing rainfall patterns, deforestation and wetland clearance for agriculture, soil erosion from farmland, cultivation near riverbanks, and the construction of structures along the lakeshore have all played a role in altering the natural hydrology of the region.

The decline in the annual flood events has highlighted the importance of conserving and restoring these seasonal wetlands. Efforts to preserve these habitats now involve a combination of traditional knowledge and modern conservation practices. Communities are increasingly recognizing the need to protect the wetlands and their associated biodiversity. Local initiatives may include reforestation programs, the establishment of protected areas, and the implementation of sustainable agricultural practices to minimize soil erosion and pollution.

In summary, the culture of conserving seasonal wetlands during and after rainy seasons is deeply rooted in the traditions and livelihoods of communities in areas where permanent freshwater is limited. These wetlands are valued for their contributions to water supply, food security, and biodiversity. While facing various challenges, the recognition of their importance has sparked conservation efforts to ensure the sustainable use and preservation of these vital ecosystems for future generations.

Chapter 4
Land and Agriculture

The Lake Victoria region is rich in diverse cultures and communities, each with their unique traditional practices and beliefs related to land cultivation and agriculture. This chapter delves into the role of traditional cultures in shaping land use patterns, farming techniques, and agricultural systems in the region. By exploring the customs, rituals, and knowledge passed down through generations, we gain insights into the sustainable practices and deep connection between communities and their lands.

The Role of Kings and the Authorities of Elders in Food and Agriculture

In traditional societies around the Lake Victoria Basin, the role of kings and authorities of elders in food and agriculture was of great significance. This section explores the influence and responsibilities of kings and elders in land management, conservation, and agricultural practices.

The Kabaka of Buganda:

In Buganda, all the land traditionally belonged to the Kabaka, the king of Buganda Kingdom. The Kabaka was regarded as the chief land custodian, and his subjects occupied and protected the land on his behalf. The Kabaka's patronage system ensured that his subjects obeyed his call to carry out agricultural activities. The system in Buganda was highly advanced compared to other ethnic communities in the region.

Land Conservation by Decrees:

The Kabaka enforced land conservation measures through decrees. He would call upon his subjects to carry out specific actions to curb soil erosion and increase food production. These decrees were promptly executed, as it was considered deviant to go against the Kabaka's edict. For instance, the Kabaka would order the digging of trenches on farms and the planting of trees to control soil erosion by wind. Grass bands of pasperum and napier grass types were also planted under the Kabaka's orders. The local administration, known as Obotangole, ensured that disobedience was punished, often through imprisonment.

Basoga and the Kyabazinga Kingdom:

Similar to Buganda, the Basoga community in Uganda was ruled through kingship. The Kyabazinga Kingdom had chiefs who collected royalties and tributes on behalf of the king. Under the chiefs, there were junior chiefs called Mutala, who further appointed individuals known as Kisoko. These officials played a crucial role in land control and management, ensuring the implementation of agricultural practices for the benefit of the community.

Luo, Suba, and Bunyala Elders:

In the Luo, Suba, and Bunyala communities of Kenya, land control powers were vested in the elders. Although not as entrenched as Kabakaism, the elders held authority in decision-making regarding land. The baraza of elders, known as "Okebe" or "Ogai" among the Luo, would convene to make important land-related decisions. Taboos and cultural beliefs were preached to the population, emphasizing the importance of conservation. Disobeying these rules and regulations could result in banishment from the community. The philosophy and traditions of these ethnic groups were imparted to younger generations through storytelling and oral traditions.

The role of kings and authorities of elders in food and agriculture played a crucial part in land management and conservation in the Lake region. The influence and power of the Kabaka of Buganda and the authorities of elders in other communities ensured the implementation of sustainable agricultural practices and the preservation of traditional land management systems. The reverence and respect given to these figures in society contributed to the successful conservation of land and the passing on of agricultural traditions to future generations.

The Traditional Role of Women in Land and Agriculture

In addition to the roles of kings and authorities of elders, women also played a significant role in land and agriculture in traditional societies around the Lake Victoria Basin. Their responsibilities extended beyond physical labor and encompassed the transmission of cultural taboos and the enforcement of customary practices related to land use.

Instilling Taboos and Cultural Practices
Women, as mothers and caretakers, were instrumental in instilling cultural taboos and traditional practices related to land and agriculture in the minds of the younger generation. They played a vital role in passing down knowledge about the sacredness of certain areas, the proper ways of cultivation, and the consequences of violating established norms.

Adjudication and Enforcement
In situations where there were land disputes or conflicts, the elders would often act as arbitrators, and they would involve the youths in enforcing their judgments. Women played a supportive role by reinforcing the decisions made by the elders and ensuring that the rules were followed. This collective effort minimized corruption and ensured a fair resolution of land-related issues.

Women's Taboos and Consequences
Specific taboos were imposed on women regarding land and agricultural activities. For example, Wasinga women were prohibited from digging the soil, except in designated fields for cultivation purposes. If a woman violated this taboo, severe consequences

were believed to occur, such as spontaneous abortion if pregnant, cracking of pottery during firing, giving birth to non-human or disabled children, or having the top layer of skin peeled off (oluhyola). These taboos served as a deterrent and reinforced the importance of adhering to cultural norms.

Protection of Sacred Areas

Certain pieces of land or grounds were set aside for traditional rituals and were considered sacred. It was strictly forbidden for anyone to enter these areas without permission from the concerned authorities. The consequences for violating this cultural tradition were believed to be severe, ranging from sexual impotence, mental illness, transformation into stones or wild animals, to madness. These severe consequences acted as a powerful deterrent, ensuring that the sanctity of sacred areas was preserved.

Overall, women played an integral role in maintaining cultural practices and taboos related to land and agriculture. Through their nurturing role as mothers and their participation in the enforcement of customary norms, they contributed to the preservation of traditional knowledge, the conservation of sacred areas, and the sustainability of land use practices. Their active involvement in land and agricultural matters helped maintain social order and the interconnectedness between culture, women, and the land.

The Traditional Methods of Food Production and Preservation

In various communities around the Lake Victoria Basin, traditional methods of food production and preservation played a crucial role in ensuring the availability of food throughout the year. These methods were often developed over generations, adapted to local environments, and guided by indigenous knowledge and practices.

Tilling the Land:

One common method of land cultivation was tilling the land.

Communities such as the Kerewe people utilized this technique to prepare the soil for planting. Tilling involved breaking up the ground using hand tools or simple implements like hoes. The soil was loosened and turned over to create a suitable seedbed for planting crops. Tilling helped to control weeds, improve soil aeration, and enhance water penetration.

Ridges and Ties:

Another traditional method employed by communities like the Kerewe was the creation of ridges with ties, known as "amafule." This technique involved shaping the soil into raised ridges, often with the help of ropes or cords (ties). The ridges provided several benefits, such as improved drainage, increased soil moisture retention, and prevention of soil erosion. Additionally, the raised beds facilitated root development and enhanced the growth of crops in regions with heavy rainfall or waterlogging.

Buds and Amakotole:

In addition to tilling and creating ridges, communities also employed the use of buds and amakotole for food production. Buds were small mounds of soil where crops like vegetables, legumes, or tubers were planted. These mounds allowed for better drainage and improved aeration of the soil around the plants' roots. The use of buds helped optimize growing conditions, especially in areas with clayey or poorly drained soils.

Amakotole, on the other hand, referred to specialized planting holes or pits. These pits were dug at specific intervals and depths, and they served various purposes depending on the community's needs. Amakotole were used for planting crops like maize, beans, or yams. The holes provided a concentrated area for planting seeds or seedlings, allowed for better moisture retention, and offered protection against pests and diseases.

Preservation Techniques:

To ensure food security and prevent spoilage, traditional communities employed various methods of food preservation.

These methods included sun-drying, smoking, fermenting, and storing in specialized structures like granaries or underground pits. Sun-drying involved laying out harvested crops in the sun to remove moisture, while smoking used the application of smoke to prevent the growth of microorganisms. Fermentation was employed for preserving foods like grains or vegetables, enhancing their shelf life and nutritional value.

Special structures like granaries or underground pits provided protection against pests, rodents, and environmental factors. These storage facilities were often constructed with materials like wood, thatch, or mud, and were designed to maintain cool temperatures and proper ventilation, thus extending the shelf life of stored food.

These traditional methods of food production and preservation were based on centuries of observation and experimentation, taking into account the local ecological conditions and cultural practices. They contributed to the sustainability of food systems, allowing communities to thrive and maintain food security throughout the year.

On the flat tilled land, communities like the Kerewe cultivated a variety of crops suited to the specific conditions. Among the crops grown were millet, busoso (sorghum), simsim (sesame), obwonzya (pumpkin), and other creeping crops. These crops were chosen for their ability to adapt to the flat terrain and thrive in the fertile soil.

The inclusion of creeping crops in the flat tilled land served multiple purposes. Firstly, these crops helped to mitigate soil erosion by providing ground cover and reducing the impact of heavy rains on the exposed soil. The sprawling nature of the creeping crops helped to stabilize the soil and prevent its loss through erosion.

On the ridges created with ties (amafule), different crops were planted to take advantage of the raised beds and improved soil drainage. Crops such as cane sugar, sweet potatoes, iwawuhoy (a local variety of beans), nandere (a leafy green vegetable), and similar crops were grown on these ridges. The ridges provided better aeration and moisture management, allowing these crops to flourish in the slightly elevated and well-drained conditions.

Within the specialized planting holes or pits known as amakotole, specific crops were cultivated. One such crop was paddy mambulumbul, a variety of rice. The introduction of rice to the island of Kerewe can be traced back to 1893 when the chief's son brought the crop from Mwanza, specifically from the Arab settlement of Kayenze. This new crop brought from outside the community expanded the agricultural diversity and added an additional food source for the people of Kerewe.

The introduction of rice cultivation showcased the exchange of agricultural knowledge and practices between different communities and regions. It highlights how the movement of people and trade routes facilitated the transfer of crops and cultivation techniques, leading to the adoption of new crops in the local agricultural systems.

Overall, the traditional cultivation practices of the Kerewe people involved the utilization of different types of land and the selection of crops suited to each specific area. By diversifying their crop selection and adapting cultivation techniques to the local environment, communities like the Kerewe were able to ensure food security and sustain their agricultural practices for generations.

The Traditional Methods of allocation of Land for Grazing and other uses

In the traditional communities around the lake, the allocation of land for grazing animals was a well-structured and regulated process. Each clan recognized the importance of preserving grazing areas for their domesticated animals, such as cows, goats, and sheep, and took measures to ensure that they grazed in designated locations.

Among the Kerewe people, a unique practice was followed to control the grazing activities of their animals. Every animal, whether it was a cow, goat, or sheep, would have akasanzo tied around its mouth. Akasanzo acted as a muzzle, preventing the animal from opening its mouth to graze on any grass or plant. This practice allowed the Kerewe to regulate and manage the grazing patterns of their animals more effectively.

To further enforce grazing regulations, specific paths called enkondo were designated for the animals to travel from their stables to the grazing lands. These paths served as corridors for the animals, ensuring that they moved directly to the designated grazing areas without trespassing on other lands. The enkondo paths were well-defined and maintained, emphasizing the importance of adhering to the designated routes and protecting other areas from being grazed upon.

The traditional chiefs or clan leaders played a crucial role in overseeing the allocation and management of grazing lands. They enforced strict rules and regulations to ensure that economic activities other than animal grazing were not carried out in these designated areas. This meant that people were prohibited from using these lands for farming, construction, or any other purpose unrelated to grazing.

The allocation of specific grazing lands and the implementation of these measures demonstrated the recognition of the importance of preserving the grazing areas for the well-being and sustenance of the domesticated animals. By designating and protecting these areas solely for grazing, the traditional communities ensured that their animals had access to sufficient and suitable vegetation while preventing overgrazing and degradation of other lands.

These traditional methods of allocating land for grazing not only ensured the proper management of grazing resources but also fostered a sense of communal responsibility and cooperation among the community members. By adhering to these practices, the clans were able to sustainably utilize their resources and maintain the delicate balance between human activities and the needs of their domesticated animals.

The Traditional Methods of Land Control and Tenure

The traditional methods of land control and tenure varied among the communities in the Lake region, reflecting their unique cultural practices and beliefs. These practices played a significant role in land management and conservation.

In the Kagera region, the land tenure system followed a feudal model known as nyarubanja, which meant "great land holding tenure." Under this system, the chief or powerful landowner had rights over various plantations and the people who worked on them. The community members served as a source of labor on the nyarubanja, and individuals were allowed to use and take care of the land on behalf of the recognized owner. Although the owner had discretionary powers over the land, mismanagement was uncommon because the owners and their children had a deep connection to the land. The owner maintained control over the user rights and could restrict activities such as grazing goats and cattle. Additionally, valuable timber trees like mvule or imusizi belonged to the owner and could only be harvested with the owner's permission.

On the Kenyan side of the lake, land ownership was based on ancestral beliefs and held by clans and families. Land was passed down from fathers to their sons through the mothers. When a woman got married, her husband would allocate a portion of land for her to till. In the event of her death without a son, the land would be shared among the surviving wives or the sons of the husband. The woman and her sons would retain control over the allocated land.

However, with changes in the land tenure system, traditional land management practices have been adversely affected. In Uganda, for example, recent laws have favored tenants rather than landlords, shifting the balance of power and control over land. This shift has weakened the inclination to conserve land, as neither the tenants nor the landlords have clear responsibilities for its management. The diminishing respect for traditional practices and the loss of soil fertility and other environmental challenges experienced in Buganda are intricately linked.

The shift in land tenure systems and the diminishing influence of traditional practices have resulted in challenges in land management and conservation. It is important to recognize and understand the historical context and cultural significance of traditional land control methods to develop effective strategies for sustainable land use and conservation in the Lake region.

The Traditional methods of Land Tenure Policy and Conservation

The traditional methods of land tenure policy and conservation varied among the communities in the Lake Victoria region, reflecting their unique cultural practices and beliefs. These practices played a significant role in soil fertility management, erosion control, and sustainable land use.

In the Kagera region, traditional methods of soil conservation included planting traditional trees such as omujuna (Recinus communis) within banana farms to control soil erosion. Banana stems were used as mulch to enhance soil fertility. Shifting cultivation practices allowed open lands to remain fallow periodically for regeneration. Kraal manure, banana peelings, and weeds were used as compost to fertilize the farms. Mixed farming and intercropping of maize and bananas were common, and grass mulching was practiced to retain soil moisture.

Among the Baganda community, traditional conservation methods included mulching (okubika ensuku) and pruning banana plants (okusaliva olukusu). Women played a vital role in fulfilling these responsibilities and imparted these practices to younger generations. Mulching, pruning, and composting techniques were taught to girls at designated places such as gwatiro or banana peeling areas. However, these traditions have declined due to changes in the school system, increased urbanization, and the influence of mass media. The transformation of land tenure systems has made it challenging to enforce traditional soil conservation methods, leading to the loss of soil fertility and environmental degradation.

Similar practices were observed among communities on the Kenyan side of the lake, where intercropping, crop rotation, mulching, terracing, and the use of mature cow dung were common methods for soil fertility and erosion control.

The Kerewe people preserved their soil by allowing it to fallow and decompose foliage, and they enriched the soil by adding ashes and animal dung. They also grew specific plants like amalegea to fertilize their fields and cultivated sisal plants, reeds, and grasses like mabingobingo to protect their fields from erosion and damage by animals.

However, the abolition of kingdoms in Uganda in 1966 and the formation of Ujamaa villages in Tanzania had significant impacts on traditional land management and conservation practices. The scaling down of traditional authorities and the introduction of new governance systems disrupted the traditional supervision of the environment. Indigenous settlement patterns were disrupted, and local people became alienated from their natural resources, leading to poor resource management practices. Colonial governance systems also encouraged soil conservation methods but often resulted in the displacement of indigenous communities and the exploitation of natural resources by foreign investors.

To ensure sustainable land use and conservation, it is crucial to recognize and respect the cultural practices and traditional land tenure systems of local communities. This includes integrating traditional knowledge and practices into modern land management approaches, promoting community participation, and implementing policies that support the preservation of cultural traditions and sustainable resource use.

The Role of Spiritual Functions in Land Conservations

Spiritual functions play a significant role in land conservation among many ethnic groups in East Africa. These communities have a deep connection to their land, considering it sacred and imbued with spiritual significance. The conservation efforts carried out by these communities are often driven by the desire to maintain the spiritual functions and integrity of the land.

The Basoga people of Uganda, for instance, hold certain natural resources such as trees, stones, caves, and swamps in high reverence. These locations become sacred spots that are respected and protected by the community. The presence of caves, large trees, and stones in these areas holds great religious significance, and they are regarded as dwelling places for spirits. The Basoga people believe in seeking permission from spiritual figures like emandwe, including kubale, mukama, and kigehnu, before interfering with or accessing these sacred sites. The fear of violating taboos and superstitions associated with these places helps maintain their conservation. This preservation of sacred sites allows vegetation to thrive, providing habitats and food sources for various animals. Additionally, the protected vegetation can produce herbs that are used for medicinal purposes.

The Luo community in Kenya also follow a similar tradition. They gather for various ritual meetings under significant trees and hold ceremonies at specific locations such as hills, riverbanks, lakeshores, cultural wrestling places, and sites associated with supernatural incidents. These sites serve as venues for rain-making ceremonies, cleansing rituals, and other important cultural practices. The management of these sites is based on their sacredness, and taboos are enforced to ensure that they are not disturbed or desecrated. The presence of these taboos safeguards the vegetation in these areas, providing a thriving ecosystem that supports biodiversity and sustains traditional practices. Examples of such sacred sites include Luanda Magere stone in Kano, Simbi Nyaima in Kendu Bay, Nyamgondho wuod Ombare in Gwassi, and Kit Mikayi in Seme.

In summary, the spiritual functions associated with the land play a crucial role in land conservation efforts. The recognition of the sacredness of certain locations and the belief in the presence of spirits and supernatural beings within these areas instills a sense of reverence and respect for the natural environment. The preservation of these sacred sites ensures the protection and flourishing of vegetation, wildlife, and cultural practices, including the use of medicinal herbs derived from these conserved areas.

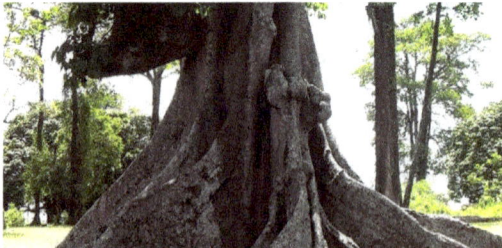

Plate 4: Nakayima Tree of Mubende Hill, Uganda

Preservation and Restoration of Food crops and Seeds

The preservation and restoration of food crops and seeds have been an integral part of traditional agricultural practices among ethnic groups such as the Luos, Suba, and Samia. Within these communities, women held the important role of being the custodians of seeds, responsible for ensuring the availability of seeds for future planting seasons. They possessed extensive knowledge about growing, processing, and storing seeds and food, which they acquired through intergenerational transmission.

In the traditional agricultural practices of these communities, various types of food crops and their seeds were carefully preserved. Some of the commonly found indigenous Luo foods and seeds included:

Millet: Millet is a drought-tolerant grain that has long been cultivated and consumed by the Luo community. Women played a key role in preserving millet seeds, ensuring their availability for subsequent planting.

Sorghum: Another staple crop among the Luo, sorghum provided sustenance and was stored in granaries. Women possessed the knowledge of selecting, processing, and storing sorghum seeds for future planting and consumption.

Beans: Different varieties of beans, such as cowpeas and kidney beans, were important protein sources in the traditional Luo diet. Women knew how to harvest and store bean seeds, ensuring a constant supply for planting and consumption.

Sweet potatoes: Sweet potatoes were a vital food crop that could be stored for an extended period. Women would carefully select healthy sweet potato tubers as seeds for the next planting season, ensuring the continuity of their cultivation.

Cassava: Cassava, a starchy root crop, played a significant role in the traditional food system. Women were responsible for selecting disease-free cassava stems to propagate and preserve the crop for future planting and consumption.To ensure the longevity of these food crops and seeds, traditional storage techniques were employed. Women utilized various methods, including drying, threshing, winnowing, and storing in special containers or granaries. They knew how to maintain optimum storage conditions, such as proper ventilation, protection against pests and rodents, and avoiding moisture that could cause spoilage.

The preservation and restoration of food crops and seeds were vital for food security and sustainability within these communities. The knowledge and skills passed down through generations by women ensured the continuous availability of diverse crops, enabling communities to adapt to changing environmental conditions and maintain their traditional food systems.

English	Dholuo	Botanical
Potatoes	*Rabuon*	*Ipomoea batatus*
Pumpkins	*Budho*	*Curcubita pepo*
Sorghum	*Bel*	*Sorgum vulgare*
Millet	*Kal*	*Eleusine corocana*
Maize	*Oduma*	*Zea mays*
Sesame	*Nyim/Simsim*	*Pennisetum Americana*
Beans	*Oganda*	*Gna unguiculata*

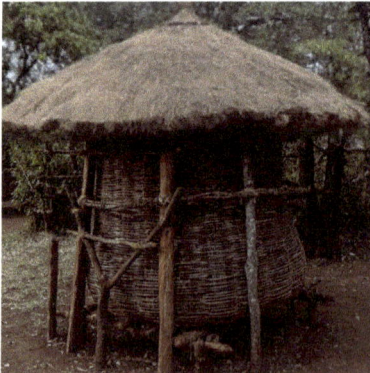

Plate 5: A traditional Luo Granary (Dero) for cereal storage

In addition to the previously mentioned food crops and seeds, there were other types of seeds that were preserved through natural means in the traditional agricultural practices of various East African ethnic groups.

The consumption of fruits, such as guava and pumpkin, resulted in the seeds being expelled through the animals' defecation. This natural process allowed the seeds to grow and propagate in a diverse range of environments. The animals, particularly hippos, played a role in dispersing the seeds through their feces, contributing to the natural growth of these plants.

For certain food crops like sorghum, millet, and cowpeas, a common preservation method involved drying them out in the field. Harvested plants were hung on a rope tied between two poles, allowing them to dry in the sun. Once dried, the crops were shaken to remove the pods or cobs, and the seeds were preserved and stored for future use.

Different seeds were conserved in various ways based on their characteristics and storage requirements. Food crops like maize, millet, and beans were harvested from the fields and separated from their respective cobs or pods. The grains were then dried in the sun before being stored in large pots or guards. To protect them from pests, the grains were dusted with ash, which acted as a natural deterrent.

Among the Banyala community, similar preservation methods were employed, but with the use of ash made from goat and sheep droppings. Storage facilities included pots specifically for planting seeds, as well as large baskets called "indaji" capable of storing multiple sacks of grains. These baskets were coated with cow dung both inside and outside to maintain the recommended temperature and protect the grains from pests. Maize and millet were sometimes retained on the cobs and pods, dried in the sun, and stored in woven granaries for daily consumption.

The traditional storage facilities, such as granaries and large pots, ensured that food crops could be preserved from one season to another while maintaining their taste. To prevent weevil attacks, layers of grass called "modhno" and "angw'e" were placed at the bottom of the granaries. Seeds for the next planting season were selected, dried, dusted with wood ash, and stored separately.

Maize seeds were often tied above cooking stoves, where the smoke from the firewood made it difficult for weevils to attack them. Other seeds, like beans and green grams, were dusted with ash and stored in large pots called "da." Groundnuts, with their hard outer covering, did not require any treatment and were hung over house roofs and granaries for preservation, remaining viable until the following planting season without being susceptible to pests.

To ensure surplus production and further conservation, marsh cultivation was practiced. It was customary for every household to have at least one granary, as it was associated with taboos. The culture of preserving crops in granaries was ingrained in the people, and all grains set aside as seeds for the next season were kept in the house of the eldest wife for enhanced protection and conservation.

In addition to seed preservation, meat preservation techniques were also employed. Meat, known as "ring'o," was preserved with honey ("mar kich") and buried in the soil in a large pot called "dak." This method, known as "kurwa" among the Luos, helped preserve the meat for extended periods. Another method of meat preservation involved drying it, resulting in a dry meat delicacy known as "aliya," which was served on special occasions to special individuals within the Luo community.

Traditional ways of Livestock Keeping and Utilization

In the traditional practices of the communities around the Lake Region, such as the Luos, livestock keeping was an integral part of their way of life alongside farming and fishing. Owning large herds of livestock was considered a symbol of wealth and prestige within the community.

To protect the livestock, a cattle boma, known as "kul," was constructed in a designated area within the homestead. This enclosed space provided a secure environment for the animals, shielding them from external threats. During the night, smaller animals like sheep and goats were kept inside huts to ensure their safety against predators and adverse weather conditions. Dogs played a crucial role in guarding the livestock, especially during nighttime, as they kept watch for potential thieves, raiders, or wild animals. Cats were also kept to help control rats and snakes, keeping the homestead free from these pests.

The availability of abundant grass and vegetation in the area provided ample grazing resources for the livestock. As there were no tools like machetes or pangas for slashing grass, the livestock were utilized to maintain the cleanliness of the homestead by allowing them to feed on the grass, naturally managing its growth.

Livestock held significant value and were not slaughtered indiscriminately. They were primarily utilized for sacrifices and cleansing rituals. As such, they were regarded as valuable assets that required careful preservation. Livestock species like goats, sheep, and hens were among the animals that held cultural and symbolic significance. Unless they died suddenly or accidentally, they were only killed during specific sacrificial ceremonies or on special occasions when they were needed for food.

The selective and intentional use of livestock for sacrifices and communal feasts reflected the deep cultural and traditional beliefs associated with these animals. Their utilization served as a way to honor and connect with spiritual and ancestral realms, reinforcing the interconnectedness between humans and animals within the community.

Chapter 5

Traditional Methods and Practices of Preserving Forests, Trees and Medicinal Plants

Conservation of Forests, Trees and Natural Vegetation

Conservation of forests, trees, and natural vegetation has been an integral part of various cultural practices and beliefs. Different communities have developed traditional methods to ensure the sustainable use and preservation of these valuable resources. Here, we explore some of the traditional practices employed by the Haya and Luo people, as well as the establishment of protected forests in the Ugandan kingdom.

Among the Haya people, forests and trees were considered communal property, overseen by the chief. The community members were allowed to collect firewood, timber, and medicinal plants from the forests with the chief's permission. This system enabled the thriving of forests such as Kinshasa, Kaneohe, Tijuana, and Lukens. By regulating tree-cutting activities, the Haya people ensured the preservation of these vital natural resources.

In Uganda, the Kabaka's government took initiatives to establish forests like Vuruga and Walumwanyi within the kingdom. These forests primarily consisted of timber trees and were respected by the community, leading to their preservation in their natural state. The cutting of trees in these forests required permission from the relevant authorities working on behalf of the Kabaka, ensuring sustainable management and conservation.

The Luo people had their unique approach to forest

conservation. During the rainy seasons (Chiri), they refrained from interfering with the forests, allowing for natural restoration. Certain trees held significant importance and were safeguarded from indiscriminate cutting. The Ochol tree, known for its medicinal properties, and the Oturbam tree, valued for timber and shade, were revered and protected. Additionally, the Luo people used some trees, such as Ojuok (Euphorbia), Njaga (Opuntia), and Siala (Markhamia platycalyx), as natural fences, which further promoted their conservation.

Selective cutting was practiced among the Luo, with only mature trees being harvested. Trees like the Ficus species were considered sacred and were not to be cut, as they served as shade during indigenous religious meetings and sacrificial ceremonies. For example, the Ficus tree in Got Nyajsure in Nyakach, Kenya, held significant cultural and religious importance, serving as a major site for sacrifices.

In addition to their cultural significance, trees and natural vegetation were recognized for their environmental benefits. The village elder, known as Ogai, played a crucial role in protecting natural vegetation and forests, acknowledging their contribution to the beauty of the earth. Certain fields were designated as grazing areas, while others allowed specific grasses to flourish for thatching houses. The natural vegetation also served as habitats for wildlife and supported diverse ecosystems.

Herbalists and medicine men held a special interest in forest conservation. They maintained specific forests dedicated to propagating medicinal plants, acting as traditional gene banks for certain tree species. In case of natural forest destruction caused by fire or drought, these specialists would release seeds from their cultivated plants to help restore the population.

Certain Luo traditions involved selecting trees for canoe or boat making through a ceremonial process. A chicken would be tied to a prospective tree and left to sleep there overnight. If the chicken survived, the tree could be felled for boat-making. However, if the chicken was eaten, it was believed that using the tree would bring harm and destroy many lives.

Furthermore, the Luo people conserved specific forests for funeral rites known as tero buru. Similar to the Hebrew culture's scapegoat ritual, these ceremonies were performed in the forest to cleanse sins and honor the deceased. In the past, conservation regulations were relatively lenient as trees were abundant compared to the settled population in the vicinity.

These traditional methods and practices highlight the deep-rooted cultural connections and the intrinsic value placed on forests, trees, and natural vegetation. They demonstrate the early recognition of the need for sustainable resource management and the preservation of biodiversity for future generations.

Norms and Special Socio-cultural Practices

To ensure the conservation of forests and trees, traditional chiefs took on the responsibility of protecting specific forests on behalf of their subjects. Each village had its designated social forest, serving various purposes such as providing hiding places during times of conflict and serving as sacred sites for clan totems and altars. Additionally, trees were grown within these forests for domestic uses, such as firewood. Moreover, households were encouraged to plant trees within their homesteads, shambas (farms), or other socio-culturally significant locations.

The Kerewe people held deep respect for trees and followed strict guidelines when it came to cutting them down. Certain trees, such as omuchwele, omuhnda, omuzule, and omwitunge, received maximum attention and were not to be indiscriminately felled. Special permission from the chief or other relevant authorities was required to do so. It was believed that anyone who cut down omuchwele without appropriate authority would suffer from illness, madness, transformation into a wild animal or child, and would be required to perform a special annual ritual. Felling omuzule was also strictly regulated, as it was a royal tree used to make chiefs' chairs and had medicinal value. Hills belonging to chiefs were covered with dense forests as a symbol of their authority.

Social institutions, including chiefdoms (ubukama), special

delegates to chiefs (omusiba), chief's assistants (mwanagwa), chief's militia (warugaruga), traditional elders and sages, and selected active youth (abasigazi), played a vital role in protecting and safeguarding the forests. The Kerewe elders still recall famous forests such as Rubya, Bumbire, Negoma, Lyamakoligo, Mukigagi, Gallu, Kikonde, Kikongora, Kifwa (Nabafwa), Masonga, Chamuhunda, Kabuhunzi, and Ibanga Iya BAtumba, which were highly valued and protected.

Unfortunately, the disappearance of many of these forests can be attributed to the abolition of chiefdoms and the rapid population growth on the island, particularly during the villagization (Ujamaa) process. Colonial governments also played a role in deforestation through their policies, as they taught and enforced clearing of forests (known as Kandukandu). In some instances, tree felling was done to combat the tsetse fly, ticks, and rinderpest. Although it had positive effects in controlling the spread of diseases, it also instilled a mindset of boldness in clearing vegetation and trees. People were led to believe that these pests were always associated with trees, especially dense forests. As a result, cattle herders developed a strong aversion to afforestation.

Taboos were prevalent in Buganda, discouraging the cutting of certain tree species or trees in specific locations of cultural significance. Some forests in the kingdom were believed to be guarded by spirits and gathering firewood from these forests was considered a severe threat to life. The exclamation "okatutyabidde!" is still widely used in Buganda, indicating that someone has invited great disaster by bringing firewood. Taboos were also established to prevent excessive deforestation, which was believed to lead to delayed rainy seasons.

Certain tree species held cultural, medicinal, and industrial importance in Buganda, and their felling was restricted to protect them. Some of these species include:

Musambya	Markhamia lutea was the main species used for building poles
Mpewere	Piptadeniastrum Africana was used in carpentry and barks was to cure a disease known as "kigalanga"
Nkikimbo	The powder from the bark was sniffed to treat flu
Jirikiti	This tree was used for soil replenishment and as a cure for nausea. It was also used for de-worming children. The tree is used as a site of disposing animal carcasses especially dogs
Mugavu	The bark of Albizi coriaria was used in preparing a concoction for bathing babied (kyogero) to prevent them form getting skin rash (ennoga)
Mutulika	The leaves of this tree were boiled and used to cure measles
Lukoma	This was used for construction
Kayukiyuki	Lantana camara was used to cure cough
Muwafu	Canarium schweinfurthii provided incense (sap) for worship in addition to fruits
Mululuza	Vernonia amygdalena was and is still widely used to cure malaria
Musaali	Synmphonia globulifera was use to cure various diseases
Omunyenye	Zanthroxylum sp. Was used for timber and to cure disease known as "ekyoka" (abdominal pain)
Nnongo	Albizia zygia was used to cure paralysis. It also provide good timber
Musizi	MAesopsis eminii was a cure of paralysis and a source of timber

In addition to the aforementioned practices, Buganda also valued several species of fruit trees, including Muyembe (Manigera indica), Ffene (Artocarpus heterophyllus), and Mutugunda (Vangueria apiculata). These fruit trees held significance not only for their edible produce but also for their medicinal properties.

Muyembe, known for its succulent fruits, had bark and leaves that were commonly used in traditional medicine. To create a soothing cough mixture, the bark and leaves of Muyembe were boiled, harnessing their therapeutic qualities. The resulting concoction was believed to alleviate coughs and respiratory ailments, providing relief to those in need.

Ffene, also known as the jackfruit tree, was esteemed for its large, flavorful fruits. The juicy, golden flesh of the ffene was a favorite among locals, and its sweet taste made it a cherished addition to various culinary delights.

Mutugunda, another notable fruit tree in Buganda, bore small, round fruits that were treasured for their unique flavor. The fruits were often consumed fresh or used in the preparation of jams and preserves, adding a distinct and delectable taste to these homemade delicacies.

These fruit trees not only contributed to the culinary diversity of Buganda but also played a vital role in traditional medicine, showcasing the deep connection between nature, culture, and health in the region. The utilization of Muyembe's bark and leaves for cough remedies exemplifies the resourcefulness of the Buganda people in harnessing the healing properties of their natural surroundings.

The Luos, Suba, and Samia communities exhibited a strong commitment to the conservation of forests, recognizing their importance for ecological balance and cultural significance. Prominent forests such as Got Ramogi, Gwassi Hills, and the Samia Hills were held in high regard and safeguarded by these communities.

Among the Sukuma people, specific trees were designated for different purposes, highlighting their meticulous approach to resource management. Whenever a member of a clan desired to cut down a tree, they would respectfully approach the local Mkami (Chief) and request permission. The Mkami played a crucial role in assessing the intended use and determining the appropriate type and quantity of trees required.

For instance, if the applicant sought to construct a hut, the chief would consider the specific tree species needed and authorize the cutting of the suitable trees from the forest. However, the applicant would be closely monitored by the chief's askaris (guards) to ensure compliance with the granted permission. This ensured that only the necessary trees were felled, preventing unnecessary deforestation.

It was strictly forbidden to request one type of wood and then use it for a different purpose. Violating this rule, such as asking for timber wood and then using it for building poles or using wood intended for fencing for other purposes, was considered a serious offense. The Mtemi (Supreme Chief) and his administrators took great care to protect sacred forests and preserve specific types of trees from any form of exploitation.

By adhering to these regulations, the communities demonstrated their deep reverence for nature and their commitment to sustainable practices. The involvement of chiefs and their askaris in monitoring and enforcing the regulations ensured the continued preservation of sacred forests and the conservation of specific tree species, fostering a harmonious relationship between the communities and their natural surroundings.

Medicinal Plants

Among the Basoga community, the preservation and utilization of medicinal plants were entrusted to the Mutala chief and the Kisoko chief, who held the responsibility for the land and its resources. The Mutala chief, in particular, played a vital role in overseeing the conservation and harvesting of medicinal herbs. Only with his authorization could the collection of plants such as lubilizi (Venonia), kilowa (Jatrophia curcas), lukone (Euphorbia trucalli), and mukungu (Ficus sur) be carried out.

In Uganda, specifically among the Basoga people, the knowledge and practice of herbal medicine were passed down through generations of herbalists and traditional practitioners. These experts were entrusted with the task of gathering medicinal herbs and employing them for healing purposes. It was common for information about specific herbs and their uses to be shared among herbalists, ensuring that valuable knowledge was preserved and disseminated.

However, the harvesting of medicinal plants was not without its rituals and conditions. Some medicine men required individuals to remove their clothes and be naked before they were allowed to collect certain herbs. Alternatively, sacrifices in the form of chickens, sheep, or goats might be necessary prerequisites for harvesting particular herbs. Those who defied these rituals and proceeded to harvest the plants were believed to have violated spiritual doctrines, resulting in dire consequences such as the swelling of feet and, ultimately, death. This strong belief in the spiritual repercussions acted as a powerful deterrent against the reckless exploitation of medicinal resources.

As a result of these cultural practices and the fear associated with defying them, the Basoga lands remained rich and fertile. The conservation of a wide variety of plant species was achieved through this system, including medicinal trees like emiumula (Meisopsis eminii), emishambya (Markhamia lute), emijuju (Ficus sp), emigango (Senecio multicory mbosa), emikoko (Ficus elastic), kikamba, rweya, omuziku, omucharaszi, and mibafu.

The careful management of medicinal plants by the Mutala chief, the adherence to rituals and conditions during their collection, and the transfer of knowledge among herbalists contributed to the sustainable utilization of these valuable resources. By maintaining a harmonious balance between human needs and the conservation of medicinal plants, the Basoga community upheld their traditions and ensured the availability of important remedies for generations to come.

Plate 6: Samples of Herbal Medicine.

The tradition of preserving medicinal knowledge and plants was not exclusive to the Basoga community but also found among the Luo people of Kenya. In Luo culture, the knowledge of herbs and their medicinal properties was considered a closely guarded secret, known only to a select group of chosen medicine men. These medicine men would bring home already processed medicine, ensuring that the specific methods of preparation and application remained hidden.

The secrecy surrounding medicinal knowledge played a crucial role in the preservation and conservation of numerous medicinal plants within the Luo community. As the common people were unaware of which plants treated specific ailments, they were cautious about randomly plucking trees or using plants for medicinal purposes. This ensured that the medicinal plants were not overexploited, and their populations were maintained.

However, the practice of traditional medicine and the conservation of medicinal plants have faced challenges in recent times due to conflicts between Christian religious beliefs and traditional systems. Some Christian denominations view the use of traditional medicine and the appeasement of spirits associated with medicinal plants as conflicting with Christian teachings. In Uganda, there have been allegations that the appeasement of spirits linked to medicinal plants has involved human sacrifices, which is considered morally repugnant and contrary to human decency.

As a result, these arguments and conflicts have weakened traditional conservation measures and disrupted the intergenerational transfer of medicinal knowledge. The fear of being associated with practices deemed incompatible with Christian beliefs has led to a decline in the adherence to traditional conservation practices among some Luo communities. Consequently, the sustainable conservation of medicinal plants and the traditional knowledge surrounding their use have been significantly affected.

It is important to find a balance between the preservation of cultural traditions and the respect for individual beliefs and values. Efforts can be made to bridge the gap between Christian religions and traditional practices, fostering dialogue and understanding to ensure the continued conservation of medicinal plants while respecting the diverse spiritual beliefs and values of the community.

Effects of Colonial Era on Forestry

The colonial era had profound effects on forestry practices and the conservation of forest resources in many regions, including Buganda. With the arrival of colonial powers and the influence of Christianity, traditional customs and beliefs related to environmental preservation faced significant challenges. Taboos and rituals that were once respected as means of conserving the environment were often denounced as "evil" by the colonial authorities, leading to a decline in their observance.

The social systems of indigenous communities were also disrupted by the colonial presence, further impacting traditional means of transferring knowledge about conservation practices. The introduction of Western culture and values contaminated the indigenous knowledge and weakened the transmission of traditional conservation practices from one generation to another.

The traditional arrangement of forest management, which was often linked to the authority of the Kabaka institution in Buganda, crumbled under the influence of colonialism. The weakening of the Kabaka institution and the erosion of traditional practices left a void in the conservation of forests and natural resources. While recent efforts by the kingdom aim to reverse this trend, there is a need for improved environmental policies to support these initiatives effectively.

Buganda's forest resources have come under enormous pressure, particularly from commercial logging activities. Forests like Mabira and Mpanga in Uganda have been heavily exploited, with the use of power-saws in commercial logging operations significantly accelerating the process of deforestation compared to traditional methods involving handsaws.

The role of Forestry Departments in East Africa as custodians of forests has been weakened, and bureaucratic procedures regarding the cutting of timber trees on private land have led to insecurity regarding ownership rights. This tenure insecurity has had negative consequences, with valuable trees like Muvule being felled at much younger ages, compromising their sustainability. It is unfortunate to note that many of the personnel responsible for managing Buganda's forests are not native to the region and may not have a strong attachment or sentiment towards the kingdom's natural resources. This situation has contributed to the irresponsible use of resources and the rapid destruction of the environment.

To address these challenges, it is crucial to prioritize the conservation and sustainable management of Buganda's forest resources. This can be achieved through the implementation of effective environmental policies, the involvement and empowerment of local communities in decision-making processes, and the promotion of education and awareness about the importance of sustainable forestry practices. Additionally, efforts should be made to restore and strengthen traditional knowledge and practices related to forest conservation, while also finding ways to reconcile traditional beliefs with Christian values and teachings.

Chapter 6
Conservation Practices

Traditional Methods of Conservation of Water and Fisheries

In the traditional communities, the conservation of water and fisheries was of utmost importance. The abundance of water resources, including the flowing rivers that fed the Lake, ensured a continuous supply of fresh water. Pollution was not a significant concern during those times, allowing the water to remain clean and unpolluted.

Among the Luo community, the control and management of lake resources followed a community-based ownership system. The individuals who owned land along the lakeshores also took on the responsibility of protecting and preserving the resources within their respective areas. The shores of the lake were divided among families, and each family utilized their designated section for agricultural purposes. For instance, specific sections of the lakeshore were known to belong to the Odongo family. This sense of ownership and responsibility motivated families to actively conserve and protect their allocated areas of the lakeshore.

However, in addition to individual ownership, there was also a collective responsibility for the conservation of resources. The "ogai" or community elders played a vital role in ensuring the overall conservation and sustainable use of water and fisheries. They served as guardians of the resources, overseeing their proper management and intervening in cases where conservation practices were not adhered to. Through this combined effort of individual ownership and communal guardianship, the lakeshores and the resources they encompassed were effectively conserved, maintaining the balance and health of the ecosystem.

These traditional methods of conservation fostered a sense of stewardship and sustainability, recognizing the interconnectedness between human activities and the natural environment. The practices of responsible ownership and community guardianship ensured the preservation of water quality and the sustainable utilization of fisheries, benefiting both the present and future generations.

Traditional Methods of Preservation of the wells and springs

The preservation of wells and springs was a significant aspect of traditional practices, emphasizing the importance of these water sources for the community. Wells were constructed and owned by individuals within the community, but they were made accessible for the free use of every community member. In order to maintain the quality and sustainability of these water sources, certain preservation methods were employed.

One crucial practice was the planting and preservation of trees and vegetation in the vicinity of wells and springs. The presence of trees and vegetation around these water sources created favorable habitats for a variety of wildlife, including leopards, pythons, bees, crocodiles, and hyenas. This biodiversity played a significant role in ensuring the safety of individuals when they visited the wells. The animals acted as natural guardians, discouraging any potential mischief or misuse of the wells by humans. Traditional beliefs held that some of these wildlife species were specifically charged with the responsibility of protecting the wells against human abuse, reinforcing the importance of respecting and preserving these vital water sources.

However, with changes in land policies and practices in the region, the preservation and maintenance of wells and springs faced significant challenges. As a result, many wells and local dams began to dry up due to insufficient protection and maintenance. The destruction of recharge areas became a prominent issue, as people started cutting down trees indiscriminately. The removal of trees and other vegetation that were crucial for groundwater recharge led to the depletion and disappearance of wells over time.

These changes highlight the consequences of disregarding traditional preservation practices and the importance of sustainable land management. The loss of wells and springs due to the lack of protection and the destruction of recharge areas serves as a reminder of the need to prioritize the preservation of natural resources. By recognizing the traditional wisdom and integrating sustainable practices, communities can ensure the long-term availability and accessibility of water sources for their well-being and the well-being of future generations.

Traditional Methods of Preservation of the Rivers

Traditional methods of preserving rivers were rooted in the belief that forests within river valleys and catchment areas were integral to the well-being of the rivers and the surrounding ecosystem. These forests were considered essential as they provided suitable habitats for wildlife and played a crucial role in safeguarding the rivers themselves. As a result, cultural norms and practices developed around the preservation of these important waterways.

One significant aspect of river preservation was the prohibition of felling trees within the river valleys and catchment areas. The belief was that these forests served as vital components of the ecosystem, supporting the biodiversity of the region. Certain trees, such as the fig tree, were particularly respected and held cultural significance within river environments. The preservation of these forests ensured the continuity of suitable habitats for various wildlife species and helped maintain the overall health of the rivers.

To protect the rivers from potential threats, communities implemented measures to prevent devastating forces such as fires and human activities. Fire management was crucial, as uncontrolled fires could destroy the vegetation along the riverbanks, leading to erosion and water pollution. Traditional practices involved the careful use of fire and strict regulations to prevent accidental or unnecessary burning near rivers.

Furthermore, human activities that could negatively impact the rivers were regulated and controlled. This included restrictions on activities such as excessive fishing, dumping waste, and extracting resources that could harm the water quality or disturb the river ecosystem. The communities recognized the interdependence between their well-being and the health of the rivers, and therefore, the preservation of these waterways was a shared responsibility.

By respecting and preserving the forests within river valleys and catchment areas, communities ensured the long-term sustainability of their water sources. The cultural attachment to these rivers and the belief in their ecological importance fostered a sense of responsibility and stewardship. These traditional methods of preservation emphasized the interconnectedness between humans, wildlife, and the natural environment, serving as a reminder of the need to protect and conserve rivers for present and future generations.

Traditional Methods of Conservation of Fisheries

Traditional methods of conserving fisheries in the Lake Victoria basin encompassed a range of practices aimed at protecting fish populations and ensuring their sustainability. However, in recent times, the lake has faced significant challenges such as the proliferation of water hyacinth and the discharge of untreated municipal waste, putting immense pressure on its ecosystem. As a result, some unorthodox and harmful methods, including the use of under-gauge nets, upstream fishing, and fish poisoning, have been employed, leading to further strain on the fish populations.

In the past, traditional leadership played a crucial role in enforcing discipline and implementing measures for the benefit of the lake resources. The Mtemi (chief) of the Kerewe people, for example, held authority and responsibility in ensuring the conservation of the fisheries. This involved implementing regulations to prevent overfishing, protect breeding grounds, and manage fishing activities sustainably.

Different communities within the Lake Victoria basin also recognized the cultural and medicinal significance of certain fish species. The Baganda people, for instance, utilized specific fish species like Nkejje for medicinal purposes and cultural rituals. Nkejje was used to treat ailments such as measles (oulusense) and was an integral part of the traditional initiation ceremony into the clan (okwalura abaana). Additionally, it was utilized to address malnutrition in children, showcasing the multifaceted roles of fish beyond mere sustenance.

Selective fishing methods were employed by various communities to ensure the capture of mature fish while allowing the young fingerlings to pass through. The Baganda, for example, used woven baskets called emiya to trap fish. These traps were designed in a way that facilitated the selective capture of mature fish, promoting the growth and reproduction of the species while minimizing the impact on the overall fish population.

Furthermore, rotational systems for using landing sites were practiced by the Baganda and potentially other communities as well. This involved the periodic rotation of fishing activities among different sites, allowing for the recovery and restocking of fish populations in specific areas. By periodically shifting fishing locations, overexploitation of a single site could be avoided, giving fish populations an opportunity to replenish and sustain themselves.

However, the contemporary approach of tendering landing sites to private business individuals for financial gain, without adequate consideration for conservation, poses significant environmental risks. Such profit-oriented management practices may prioritize short-term economic interests over the long-term sustainability of the fisheries and the overall health of the lake ecosystem.

Preserving and conserving fisheries in the Lake Victoria basin requires a comprehensive and holistic approach. Efforts should include addressing pollution and invasive species, implementing sustainable fishing practices, promoting community-based conservation initiatives, and ensuring effective governance and regulation to safeguard the long-term viability of the fish populations and the ecological balance of the lake ecosystem.

Plate 7: Lake Kabaka.

In order to prevent overexploitation of fishing areas, traditional fishermen in Buganda would practice rotational fishing. After fishing from one site for a certain period, they would relocate to another area, allowing fish populations in the previous location to recover and replenish. However, the abundance and diversity of fish species in the rivers and lake of Buganda have significantly declined, with several species now facing the threat of extinction. Among the species at risk are nkolongo, nningu, semutungu, mmale, kasulubana, kisinja, nkejje, and ngege. The introduction of the Nile perch (mbuta) into the lake is believed to have played a significant role in the loss of biodiversity within the lake and its surrounding rivers.

Within the Luo community, the concept of family ownership of the beaches ensured that wetlands along the water shores were not cultivated. This protective measure helped to safeguard the breeding grounds for fish. Traditional fishing practices among the Luo did not involve destructive methods such as trawling or the use of explosives. If an underage fish was caught, it was immediately released back into the water before it could perish. Additionally, the fact that people had diverse dietary habits, not solely dependent on fish, contributed to the conservation of fish stocks in the lake. To allocate fishing areas, specific sections of the lake were designated for each ethnic group, and the responsibility of managing and conserving these areas rested with the respective communities. However, the consumption of fish has been intensified by export trade, leading to unsustainable fishing practices.

The Basoga people held a deep cultural and symbolic connection to Lake Victoria. They regarded the lake, under the authority of the Kyanazinga Kingdom, as one of their greatest cultural treasures alongside the land. The lake represented the cultural identity of the Busoga people, and its spirit was associated with transportation and blessings for the community. The Kyabazinga Kingdom exercised control over the lake, including the management of landing sites, issuance of fishing permits, and collection of revenue from fishing activities. In the past, when wetlands, swamps, and other ecosystems surrounding Lake Victoria were communally managed, they were effectively conserved. However, the current trend of assigning individual ownership of wetlands and swamps due to population growth has undermined the role of superstition and taboos as conservation tools.

The division of labor based on cultural and traditional beliefs also helped regulate the number of fishermen in the lake, preventing overfishing. Certain types of fish, such as fina and shilonge, were not commonly used as food but rather for medicinal purposes, resulting in their less frequent capture. Similarly, there were fish species, like kamongo and mbele, that were traditionally not eaten by females, leading to their reduced exploitation. Each clan had designated resting and breeding places for fish, and traditional fishing equipment was designed to ensure sustainable fisheries by targeting mature fish while sparing under-age ones. Fishing activities were conducted in different parts of the lake, such as deep waters (simbila), middle waters (olwaagati), and high waters (Nyamlela), based on the knowledge of the presence of mature fish in those areas.

The Luos and Subas, similar to their counterparts in Uganda, had comparable traditional fishing practices. However, these practices, such as using selective fishing gear like gogo and osadhi to spare under-age fish, have been declining under the influence of changing values. It was customary for Luo fishermen to return any fingerlings they accidentally caught back into the water before they died, as it was believed to bring bad omens and potential harm to the individual. Such traditional values were passed down through folk tales to instill respect for the ecosystem and its resources. Fishing was banned in the entire region from April to August, which was considered the breeding season for fish. Additionally, fishing activities conducted during recommended seasons were deliberately conducted away from wetland areas. This was done during the long rainy season when fish would come closer to the shores of the lake or migrate upstream to breed. Meanwhile, crops like maize and millet would mature in the fields, and fishermen would take several days to observe sexual rituals associated with farming practices. These events helped alleviate pressure on fisheries, resulting in high fish population and species diversity.

Overall, these traditional methods of fisheries conservation in Buganda, Luo, Suba, and Basoga communities exemplify the wisdom of indigenous practices in balancing human needs with the sustainable use and protection of natural resources.

Plate 8: A fish Landing Beach

The conservation of specific fish species held great importance in certain cultural practices. For instance, fishes like Ngenge (tilapia) and Kamongo (lungfish) were highly valued as special delicacies for welcoming and entertaining visiting in-laws. In order to preserve these species, traditional fishermen employed the use of gogo, a type of beach seine fishing gear. The gogo had a wide opening that allowed young fish to escape, ensuring that only mature fish were captured.

However, in the early 1970s, the introduction of the Nile perch, a predatory species, had a significant impact on the ecosystem of Lake Victoria. While the presence of the Nile perch itself did not directly affect the catch of other fish, the negative impact was attributed to unsustainable fishing practices. Additionally, the proliferation of water hyacinth, an invasive plant, caused the lake to become enclosed, leading to the resurgence of fish species that had previously disappeared due to lack of protection. Fishes such as mumi (Claria mossambicus), kamongo (proteptorus), okoko (Synodontis spp.), fulu (Haplochromis sp.), ningu (Laneo victorianus), fuani (Barbu sp.), mbiru (Oreochromis variabilis), and osoga (Alestes spp.) reappeared in small quantities after a prolonged absence.

This demonstrates the complex interplay between introduced species, environmental changes, and fishing practices in the dynamics of fish populations in Lake Victoria. The need for sustainable fishing practices and the conservation of diverse fish species remains crucial for the long-term health and balance of the lake's ecosystem.

The Traditional Fishing Equipment

The traditional fishing equipment used by the Sukuma people played a crucial role in promoting conservation practices. Among the commonly used fishing tools were "matete," "ihumbi," "ihongola," and "olubigo." These devices were intentionally designed to discourage massive and abusive fishing practices. Their small size and manual operation required intensive personal attention, making it difficult to engage in indiscriminate fishing. Additionally, specific instruments had restrictive functions. For example, "olubale" was specifically designed for catching a particular fish species called schilbes nembe, while "omasaku" was used for trapping mature fish only. Similarly, "ihongola ya mumugele" was meant exclusively for fishing in rivers.

In the Kerewe culture, all traditional fishing tools had limited fishing capacities, emphasizing the importance of catching fish sparingly and sustainably. For instance, the fishing boats known as "obwato bwe biku" were used by fishermen to transport their equipment and move from one location to another. These boats were intentionally small in size, allowing them to carry only a few people at a time. Consequently, the tonnage of the catch was also limited by the boat's capacity. This ensured that fishing activities remained in balance with the available resources and helped prevent overexploitation of fish populations.

Plate 9: A Traditional Fish Trap

During the dry season, when rivers would often dry up and fish became easily accessible to birds, the Kerewe people devised a method to catch and preserve the fish for their own consumption. To prevent the wastage of fish, fishermen used a plant called "omululu," which was soaked in water to create a poisonous liquid. This liquid was carefully poured into specific pockets of stagnant river water where fish were hibernating. The fishermen took precautions to ensure that the "omululu" liquid would not flow into sources of drinking water. By using this method, the Kerewe people were able to catch fish in drying rivers and avoid the loss of valuable resources.

Similarly, the Luos also employed a similar technique using a poisonous plant called "ober" (Albizia coriaria) to catch fish. The fish caught through this method were sun-dried and smoked to eliminate the poison. However, in modern times, some greedy fishermen have resorted to using deadly poisons like theodan, which poses a severe threat to both fish populations and consumers. The use of such lethal poisons has led to cases of poisoning among those who consume the contaminated fish.

Originally, the Sukuma people were not traditionally fishermen and learned the practice from the neighboring Kerewe and Zinza communities. As a result, their fishing tools and techniques resembled those of these tribes. The Sukuma primarily engaged in fishing during the rainy season when rivers flooded, causing fish to move upstream in search of fresh food. Their fishing tools, although relatively simple, were suited for fishing in rivers rather than the deeper waters of the lake.

Women in the communities also participated in fishing, particularly in lower water areas and rivers with less powerful currents. They used well-woven baskets known as "ounga" to catch fish quickly, enabling them to prepare morning meals for their children. Fishing in this manner provided a convenient and efficient way for women to contribute to their households.

The introduction of modern fishing tools and practices has had a detrimental impact on Lake Victoria, including the Ukerewe region. Modern fishnets with wider mesh sizes ranging from 1.5 to 5.5 inches have led to massive and unsustainable fishing practices on the island. Hooks and trawler nets were not commonly used as they were not selective, resulting in the overexploitation of fish populations.

For the Luos in Kenya, traditional fishing equipment included tools such as "sienyo," "ounga," "togo," "odhuro," "otete," "kira" (onduru mitudo), "bidhi," "osadhi," and "kunya" (for mumi and kamongo). These tools were used to catch larger fish. The "ober" tree was crushed and mixed with water, creating a substance that was added to the lake to intoxicate the fish and cause them to float to the surface, making them easier to catch. The effects of the "ober" dissipated quickly, allowing the fish to become active again and swim away. This method had a minimal and short-term impact on the fish and did not pollute the water.

The Traditional Fishing Boats

Traditional fishing boats played a crucial role in the fishing activities of the Kerewe, Ssese Islands, Luos, and Suba communities, each with their unique characteristics and significance.

In the Kerewe fishing tradition, the fishermen utilized "obwato bwibika" as their primary means of transportation during fishing expeditions. These boats were relatively small in size, accommodating only a limited number of people and carrying a specific tonnage of fish catch. The size limitation of these boats acted as a constraint on massive and indiscriminate fishing practices. By limiting the capacity of the boats, the Kerewe fishermen unintentionally contributed to the conservation of fish as a natural resource. The smaller boat sizes encouraged sustainable fishing practices and prevented overexploitation of fish populations.

In contrast, the traditional fishing boats used in the Ssese Islands (Kalangala) were referred to as "one man's canoes." These boats were small in size, designed to carry only one person. However, they were highly efficient and fast, enabling effective fishing operations. The Ssese fishermen relied on their individual skills and agility to navigate the waters and catch fish using these small boats. Despite their limited capacity, the Ssese boats allowed for agile maneuvering and precise fishing techniques, making them an integral part of the fishing culture in the region.

Similarly, the Luos and Suba communities also utilized small boats for their fishing activities. These boats were traditionally crafted from carefully selected trees from the forest. The construction of these boats required skilled craftsmanship, ensuring that they were sturdy and capable of withstanding the demands of fishing in the lake. These legendary fishing boats hold cultural significance and serve as reminders of the communities' traditional practices. Preserving and protecting these boats as cultural artifacts helps maintain the cultural heritage and identity of the communities.

The use of traditional fishing boats, whether the "obwato bwibika" of the Kerewe, the "one man's canoes" of the Ssese Islands, or the small boats of the Luos and Suba, exemplifies the intimate connection between the communities and their fishing traditions. These boats not only facilitated transportation and fishing but also contributed to the conservation of fish populations by imposing limits on fishing capacity. Their continued existence and preservation serve as a testament to the rich cultural and historical ties that these communities have with their aquatic environments.

The Traditional Methods of Fish Preparation and Preservation

Traditional methods of fish preparation and preservation played a vital role in ensuring a stable food supply and access to protein for communities around Lake Victoria. Fish was a staple food and consumed in various forms at most meals.

One common method of fish preservation was sun-drying. Fish would be cleaned, salted, and then spread out under the sun to dry. This process helped remove moisture from the fish, extending its shelf life and making it suitable for long-term storage. Dried fish was highly valued for its durability and convenience. It could be stored in large pots known as Degi or dokwonde, providing a readily available source of protein for households. In addition to household consumption, dried fish also had commercial value, and people engaged in barter trade, exchanging dried fish for other commodities such as cereals.

Smoking was another method used to preserve fish. Fish would be hung over a fire or placed on racks above smoldering wood or charcoal, allowing the smoke to penetrate the fish and imparting a distinct flavor. Smoked fish had a shorter shelf life compared to dried fish but was favored for its unique taste. The choice between sun-drying and smoking fish depended on individual preferences and local customs.

In Kerewe, similar to Luo culture, dried fish held significant importance as a food source. The practice of catching "dagaa" fish, a type of small sardine-like fish, was introduced to the Kerewe islands from Lake Tanganyika in Kigoma during the 1970s. Prior to this introduction, the Kerewe people relied on other types of fish for their dietary needs.

Selective consumption was practiced, meaning that people did not engage in massive fishing as seen in contemporary times. Each clan owned and fished in specific areas of the lake, and outsiders were not welcomed to intrude upon their fishing grounds. This localized ownership and fishing rights helped maintain a balanced ecosystem and sustainable fish populations.

In addition to fish, communities also relied on other sources of protein, such as cow milk, beef, and meat from both wild and domesticated animals. The abundance of wildlife in the region allowed for hunting, providing an alternative source of protein for the communities.

Overall, the traditional methods of fish preparation and preservation, including sun-drying and smoking, ensured a stable food supply and allowed communities to sustainably utilize the resources of Lake Victoria. These practices, coupled with selective consumption and localized fishing rights, contributed to the preservation of fish populations and the maintenance of a diverse protein-rich diet.

Plate 10: Fish Preparation

Traditional Method of Preserving Fish Breeding Grounds

Traditional methods of preserving fish breeding grounds were practiced by fishing clans around Lake Victoria, including the Kerewe people. One important aspect of this preservation was the protection of vegetation, particularly olwenge, which provided a favorable environment for fish breeding. Destruction of these vegetation was strictly prohibited to ensure the continued abundance of fish.

The Kerewe people recognized three fishing seasons, each corresponding to different water depths and fish behavior. During the first season, when fish were in deep water (simbila), fishing activities would focus on those areas. In the second season, fish would swim near the water surface (nymlela), allowing for fishing to be carried out there. Finally, during the third season, fish would inhabit the shallow waters (olwaagati), and fishing efforts would be directed accordingly. By following the natural patterns of fish behavior and migration, the Kerewe people ensured that fish were left undisturbed to breed during the appropriate times.

The colonial government recognized the importance of preserving fish populations and implemented fishing bans during certain periods to protect fish breeding grounds. However, over time, with the changing dynamics of the fishing industry and increased demand for fish, people began to defy these cultural practices. Fishermen started catching fish indiscriminately, even when they were in their breeding stage. This unsustainable fishing practice led to a decline in fish stocks in the lake.

Nevertheless, the Kerewe people maintained their traditional conservation practices due to their spiritual connection with certain fish species. Each clan protected specific resting and breeding areas for fish, ensuring the sustainability of fisheries. They used fishing equipment and techniques that minimized the impact on fish populations and allowed for their continued reproduction.

However, in recent times, uncontrolled and unlimited trade liberalization within the fishing industry has contributed to overfishing and the depletion of fish stocks. The domestic market has suffered from a severe shortage of fish, leading to exorbitant prices that many people cannot afford. This imbalance between supply and demand has had significant socioeconomic implications for the community, impacting their access to this vital food source.

Efforts to address these challenges and restore sustainable fishing practices are crucial. This includes implementing regulations and monitoring systems to control fishing activities, promoting responsible fishing practices, and raising awareness about the importance of preserving fish breeding grounds and maintaining healthy fish populations for the benefit of both the environment and the local communities.

Chapter 7
Biodiversity

Biodiversity played a crucial role in the lives of the communities residing in the Lake Victoria region. The preservation and conservation of various animals, fish, plants, birds, and reptiles were paramount in maintaining the balance of nature. Different clans and communities had special spiritual and cultural ties with specific species, and these connections contributed to the preservation of biodiversity.

For instance, the Kerewe people held the python in high regard, considering it holy. Killing a python was believed to bring serious calamities upon the individual and their family. Similarly, the Gwassi people revered big snakes in the Gwassi Hills, as they believed their grandfather, Kiboye, transformed into a large snake. The presence of these snakes was considered sacred, and their preservation was intertwined with the conservation of the natural resources in the hills.

The Wazigaka clan among the Kerewe people had a special cultural attachment to leopards, prohibiting their killing or mistreatment. The Waruji clan within Ukerewe Island also had cultural ties to a specific type of hyena. These cultural affiliations fostered a sense of respect and conservation for these animals, contributing to their protection within the community.

Other clans and communities had similar beliefs and practices. The Wegitwa clan, for example, refrained from touching ant bears, while the Abamilo, Abachamba, and Abayango clans would not harm baboons, wild pigs, or monkeys, respectively. The totems consisting of different animals among the Samia and Manyala communities in Kenya also played a significant role in preserving these species, providing them with safe havens where they could thrive without human predators.

Wild animals and game inhabited various habitats, including social forests, hills, ritual places, river valleys, and areas around wells. These habitats were characterized by dense forests that provided suitable and attractive environments for the fauna. The Kerewe people, understanding the importance of the biodiversity cycle, allowed it to take its natural course, maintaining biodiversity at satisfactory levels in the Lake Victoria basin.

Hunting was a common activity in Buganda, serving both as a sport and a means to obtain wild meat. Hunters utilized various tools such as nets, traps, spears, and horns for communication during hunting expeditions. Certain animals were targeted and scared into set nets, after which they were speared to death. The hunting practices were regulated to prevent the overuse and depletion of animal populations.

The Sukuma people also valued biodiversity for self-sustenance and proper maintenance. They recognized the significance of specific fauna and flora in their lives and respected and preserved their habitats. Some snakes were used in traditional dances, while others were utilized as medicines by traditional healers. These snakes would be killed, dried, and ground into powder for their medicinal properties.

In the past, the Mtemi Chief owned all the animals in his territory, and permission had to be sought to hunt. The hunters had to provide valid reasons for their hunting requests, such as hosting a party or sending away a daughter in marriage. The chief granted permission only for specific animals and closely monitored the hunting activities through his scouts. If any individual attempted to hunt without permission, they would be reported, as the community believed that the chief owned the animals on behalf of the public. This system ensured the protection of totem animals and guaranteed diversity among animal species.

The institution of "wanangwe," or sub-chiefdom, acted as a link between the public and the chiefdom. Public demands for natural resources were communicated to the chief through the "wanangwe," and the chief's decisions regarding these requests were relayed back to the public. This system aimed to ensure the justified, controlled, and proper use of the natural resources in question, contributing to the sustainable management of biodiversity.

Overall, the cultural, spiritual, and traditional practices of the communities in the Lake Victoria region played a vital role in the preservation and conservation of biodiversity. These practices fostered a deep respect for certain species, ensured sustainable use of natural resources, and maintained a delicate balance between human activities and the natural world.

Wild Animals

Elephant

The elephant, a majestic and gentle creature, held a special place in the cultural beliefs and traditions of various communities. Among these communities, such as the Baganda, the elephant was regarded as a symbol of abundance and prosperity. When an elephant passed through a village, it was believed that the food production in that village, both at present and in the following year, would be bountiful.

The sighting of an elephant wandering through the village was not taken lightly. Community members would immediately inform their cultural leaders, traditional medicine men, and the chief. A meeting would be called, and rituals would be performed to honor the presence of the elephant. It was considered a sacred event, and nobody was allowed to harm or kill an elephant without the permission of the chief.

In addition to its spiritual significance, various parts of the elephant were utilized for practical purposes. Traditional healers would make use of elephant droppings as a component in their medicinal treatments for certain diseases. The tusks and other parts of the elephant's body were considered valuable curative tools, believed to possess healing properties. Local or traditional dancers incorporated parts of the elephant's body into their performances, adding a cultural element to their artistry.

Furthermore, elephants also served as a source of sustenance.

People would consume the flesh of elephants, providing nourishment and sustenance for the community. The ivory obtained from the elephant's tusks held significant value and was highly prized. In fact, the elephant served as a totem for the Baganda people, symbolizing their identity and connection to the natural world.

Overall, the elephant's presence invoked a sense of reverence and reverence within these communities. Its association with abundance, its medicinal properties, and its practical uses contributed to the cultural significance and deep respect held for this magnificent creature.

Hyena

The hyena holds a significant place in the cultural beliefs and fears of the Sukuma and Luo communities. Even to this day, many Sukuma people continue to harbor a deep fear of hyenas due to their traditional and cultural associations. In the traditional belief system, the hyena is considered an animal ridden by witches when performing witchcraft rituals. This belief instills fear and apprehension among the community members, who view the hyena as a potential danger or threat.

Because of this cultural belief, people would actively hunt hyenas out of fear of angering or annoying witches. If there was an increase in the hyena population in a particular village, the community members would raise their concerns with their cultural and traditional leaders. A meeting would be convened, usually led by the chief or their assistant, to address the issue. During these discussions, the chief would express anger towards the witches and instruct them to hide their hyenas and prevent them from causing trouble to the community.

Similarly, among the Luo community, a hyena, known as "Ondiek," held specific cultural significance. It was believed that the Ondiek should not undergo a ritualistic cleansing ceremony called "tweyo tora." This ceremony was performed to cleanse individuals or animals from impurities or negative influences. The Ondiek, being associated with its own set of cultural beliefs and powers, was exempt from this cleansing process.

The fear and apprehension surrounding hyenas in these communities highlight the deep-rooted cultural beliefs and superstitions that shape their perceptions and interactions with wildlife. These beliefs serve as a means to explain and understand the world around them, while also influencing their behaviors and practices.

Monkeys

Monkeys, known as "Nkima" in the Baganda culture, held a special place as agents of seed dispersal and were associated with the totems of the Baganda people. The monkey's role in seed dispersal played a crucial ecological function in maintaining the diversity and balance of forest ecosystems.

Monkeys are highly mobile and agile creatures, known for their ability to move swiftly through the trees. As they moved from tree to tree, they inadvertently carried seeds on their fur and in their digestive systems. These seeds would later be deposited in different locations as the monkeys traveled, effectively dispersing them from one forest to another. This process played a vital role in the distribution and colonization of plant species, contributing to the overall health and regeneration of forest habitats.

In Baganda culture, the monkey was regarded as a totem animal, representing a particular clan or family lineage. Totems are symbolic representations of ancestral spirits or animal guides that hold a significant place in the cultural identity and beliefs of a community. The Baganda people revered the monkey as a totem animal, attributing certain qualities and characteristics to it, such as agility, intelligence, and adaptability.

The association of the monkey with the Baganda totem reflected a deep spiritual and cultural connection to the natural world. It symbolized the importance of living in harmony with nature and respecting the ecological roles played by different animals. The Baganda people recognized the monkey's role as a seed disperser and acknowledged its contribution to the ecosystem's balance and the survival of plant species.

By embracing the monkey as a totem, the Baganda people

expressed their reverence for nature and the interconnectedness of all living beings. This cultural belief system helped foster a sense of stewardship and conservation of natural resources, as people recognized the intrinsic value of preserving the habitats and biodiversity that sustained their livelihoods.

Overall, the monkey's significance in Baganda culture went beyond its ecological role as a seed disperser. It served as a symbol of ancestral heritage, a reminder of the interconnectedness of all life forms, and a representation of the community's cultural identity and values.

Bats

Bats, known as "Binyira" in some cultures, played a significant role as agents of seed dispersal. Despite their often misunderstood and mysterious reputation, bats served as valuable contributors to ecosystem health and biodiversity through their seed dispersal activities.

Bats have unique adaptations that make them well-suited for seed dispersal. Many bat species are nocturnal, meaning they are active during the night when other animals are not, allowing them to take advantage of resources that might not be available to diurnal animals. Bats also have the ability to fly, which grants them access to diverse habitats and enables them to cover large distances in search of food.

When bats consume fruits or nectar from various plants, they often ingest the seeds along with their meal. As they fly and travel between feeding sites, bats play a crucial role in dispersing these seeds. The seeds are typically small and resilient, able to pass through the bat's digestive system unharmed. When the bat eventually excretes the seeds, they are deposited in different locations, sometimes far away from the parent plant.

This seed dispersal mechanism provided by bats has several ecological benefits. First, it allows plant species to colonize new areas and expand their distribution range. By transporting seeds to different habitats, bats facilitate the establishment of plants in diverse ecosystems, contributing to the overall resilience and biodiversity of the landscape.

Additionally, bats often target fruit-bearing trees and plants that provide essential resources for other wildlife species. As bats feed on these fruits, they inadvertently create a valuable food source for other animals, including birds, monkeys, and other mammals. This ripple effect of bat-mediated seed dispersal helps sustain the interconnected web of life within an ecosystem.

In some cultures, bats hold symbolic significance and cultural interpretations. They are associated with mysticism, nocturnal activities, and the realm of the unseen. In folklore and mythology, bats often represent transformation, intuition, and the crossing of boundaries between different worlds. Their ability to navigate in the darkness and their unique ecological role as seed dispersers have given them a place in the cultural narratives and beliefs of various societies.

Overall, bats' role as agents of seed dispersion is a remarkable example of the intricate relationships between animals and plants in nature. Recognizing the importance of bats and their contribution to ecosystem health and biodiversity can foster a greater understanding and appreciation for these remarkable creatures and their vital ecological functions.

Mole Rats

The mole rat, known as "Omusu" in Buganda, held a dual significance as a source of food and as a symbol with cultural connotations. In Buganda culture, certain animals are considered totems, representing a clan or group of people, and the mole rat is one such totem for the Baganda people.

From a culinary perspective, the mole rat was recognized as edible game. It was hunted and consumed by the local communities, providing a source of sustenance and nourishment. The meat of the mole rat was valued for its taste and nutritional value, contributing to the dietary diversity of the people.

Beyond its role as a food source, the mole rat also had cultural significance in Buganda. Its behavior of burrowing underground and creating intricate pathways in the soil was recognized and appreciated by the local communities. These tunnels and channels made by the mole rat served multiple purposes.

Firstly, the mole rat's burrowing activities helped aerate the soil and improve its fertility. By creating tunnels, the mole rats allowed air to reach deeper layers of the soil, facilitating the circulation of oxygen and promoting the growth of beneficial microorganisms. This, in turn, enhanced the overall health and productivity of the soil, making it more suitable for agriculture.

Moreover, the tunnels created by the mole rats acted as conduits for moisture. During periods of rainfall, the pathways served as channels for water to penetrate the soil and reach deeper layers, ensuring better water retention and distribution. This was particularly valuable in regions with variable or limited rainfall, as the mole rat's activities helped to optimize water availability for plants and other organisms in the ecosystem.

The cultural connotations attached to the mole rat as a totem for the Baganda people reflected a deeper connection and respect for nature. It represented a shared identity and kinship with the animal, acknowledging its ecological role and the benefits it brought to the land and the community.

The significance of the mole rat in Buganda culture demonstrates the traditional knowledge and observations of the local people, recognizing the intricate relationships between animals, soil health, and agricultural productivity. By valuing and understanding the contributions of animals like the mole rat, communities could develop sustainable practices that preserved the natural environment and ensured the well-being of both humans and the ecosystem as a whole.

Porcupine

The porcupine, known as "Namunungu," holds a unique place in the cultural and natural landscape. This fascinating animal not only serves as a source of food but also possesses a remarkable defense mechanism that has medicinal properties and is valued in traditional healing practices.

As an edible game, the porcupine has been hunted and

consumed by various indigenous communities. Its meat is appreciated for its flavor and nutritional value, providing sustenance and nourishment. The hunting and preparation of porcupine meat have become embedded in cultural traditions and culinary practices, showcasing the resourcefulness and adaptability of local communities.

One of the most distinctive features of the porcupine is its quills, which are sharp, barbed spines that cover its body. These quills serve as a highly effective defense mechanism against potential predators. However, beyond their defensive role, the quills of the porcupine also possess medicinal properties that have been recognized and utilized by traditional healers.

In traditional medicine, the quills of the porcupine are used to treat various ailments. For example, the sharp thorns are believed to have healing properties for body sores (ntunuka) and certain skin rashes (kigabi). When applied properly, the quills are believed to alleviate discomfort, reduce inflammation, and promote healing. Additionally, the porcupine quills have been used to address cases of malnutrition (obwosi), potentially due to the nutritional value associated with consuming porcupine meat.

The utilization of porcupine quills in traditional medicine highlights the deep understanding and observation of local communities regarding the natural world. Through generations of experience and knowledge transfer, indigenous healers have identified the healing potential of these unique spines and incorporated them into their medicinal practices.

The cultural significance of the porcupine extends beyond its medicinal properties. In some cultures, the porcupine may hold symbolic meanings, representing qualities such as resilience, protection, or adaptability. Its presence in folklore, myths, and ceremonies often carries important lessons and teachings related to personal and communal well-being.

The porcupine's dual role as a source of sustenance and as a provider of medicinal resources exemplifies the interconnectedness of nature and culture. Indigenous communities have developed a profound appreciation for the porcupine's contributions, recognizing its ecological importance, its role in local economies, and its potential to address certain health issues.

In conclusion, the porcupine's edible game status, combined with the unique medicinal properties of its quills, has led to its integration into traditional diets and healing practices. This animal serves as a testament to the rich relationship between humans and nature, showcasing the resourcefulness and wisdom of indigenous communities in utilizing the natural world for both sustenance and healing.

Hippopotamus

The hippopotamus, known as "Nyubu" among the Baganda people, held significant cultural and practical value in their society. Not only was it considered as another source of edible game, but it also played a role in traditional medicine and agricultural practices. Similarly, among the Luos, the presence of a hippo, referred to as "Rao," was associated with specific customs and beliefs.

In Baganda culture, the hippopotamus served as a valuable resource for medicinal purposes. The Baganda believed that certain parts of the hippo, such as its bones, fat, or organs, possessed healing properties. In particular, the hippo was renowned for its ability to treat foot and mouth diseases in cattle. Traditional healers would utilize various parts of the hippo in their remedies, employing their knowledge of herbal medicine to create treatments that could alleviate these ailments in livestock.

Moreover, the dung of the hippopotamus held a special significance in Baganda agricultural practices. It was burnt as incense or used as a charm in gardens to invoke blessings and ensure a prosperous harvest. The act of burning hippo dung was believed to attract the favor of ancestral spirits or gods, bringing fertility to the land and guaranteeing abundant crops. This practice reflected the close relationship between the Baganda people, their agricultural endeavors, and the spiritual realm.

Among the Luo community, a cultural belief emerged regarding the sight of a hippopotamus, particularly for women. It was customary for women not to see a hippo, as men who skinned the animal would do so without wearing any clothes during the process. This practice was meant to respect cultural boundaries and maintain privacy within the family. Fathers-in-law would be responsible for the skinning, ensuring that their daughters-in-law were not exposed to this activity. This custom reflected the social and cultural dynamics within Luo society, highlighting the importance of modesty, respect, and adherence to established gender roles.

The significance of the hippopotamus in Baganda and Luo cultures exemplifies the intricate relationships between humans, animals, and the natural world. These beliefs and practices showcase the diverse ways in which communities have integrated the presence of hippos into their daily lives, whether through hunting for sustenance, utilizing their medicinal properties, or observing cultural customs. Such cultural connections with animals not only demonstrate the rich tapestry of African traditions but also underscore the deep reverence and interdependence between humans and the animal kingdom.

Frog

In Luo culture, the frog, known as "ogwal" and scientifically referred to as Rana tigrina, held symbolic and practical significance within their beliefs and daily lives. The frog was considered a visitor or messenger (wendo) of the house, and as such, it was treated with respect and care by the community.

Children were taught not to harm or kill frogs, as they were believed to have a beneficial role in protecting households from snakes. It was believed that if a snake fed on a frog, it would become harmless to humans. Therefore, the presence of frogs in and around the house was seen as a natural deterrent against snake bites and harm. This notion fostered a sense of coexistence between humans and frogs, as the harmless nature of frogs contributed to the safety and well-being of the community.

In addition to their role in snake prevention, frogs were associated with fertility and childbirth. It was believed that if a frog visited a house while a woman was expecting a child, she would give birth to a baby girl. This belief added a sense of anticipation and meaning to the presence of a frog, as it was seen as an auspicious sign for the gender of the unborn child.

Furthermore, frogs were regarded as indicators of weather patterns, particularly rainfall. During the dry season, if frogs were observed moving around or making more noise than usual, it was interpreted as a sign that rain was imminent. The elders in the community paid close attention to these behaviors of frogs, using them as natural predictors of forthcoming rain. This connection between frogs and rainfall demonstrated the intimate knowledge and observation of nature that the Luo people possessed, allowing them to interpret and respond to the environmental cues provided by the animal kingdom.

Additionally, the presence of a frog jumping from the bush was seen as an indication of a snake's presence near the homestead. This observation served as a warning to the community, alerting them to the potential danger and prompting them to take necessary precautions to ensure their safety.

The beliefs surrounding frogs in Luo culture reflect a deep respect for the natural world and its interconnectedness with human life. Frogs were not only seen as protectors and messengers but also as symbols of fertility, rain prediction, and environmental awareness. These cultural understandings exemplify the harmonious relationship between humans and animals, as well as the valuable wisdom that indigenous communities have gained through their observations and interpretations of the natural world.

Tortoise

In Luo culture, the tortoise, known as "opuk," held a special place as a revered creature due to its characteristics of being harmless and slow. The community nurtured a deep respect for the tortoise, and children were strictly forbidden from harming or killing it. They were taught that the tortoise should be treated with care and kindness.

One belief surrounding the tortoise was the notion that if a child killed a tortoise, it would bring harm to their grandmother. This belief served as a powerful deterrent for children, emphasizing the importance of preserving and respecting all living beings, regardless of their size or perceived significance. The symbolic association between the tortoise and the well-being of the grandmother underscored the interconnectedness and interdependence within the family unit.

The tortoise's characteristic slowness and harmless nature contributed to its elevated status in Luo culture. These traits were seen as virtues to be admired and emulated. The tortoise's deliberate and cautious movements were often regarded as wisdom in action, teaching the community the value of patience, endurance, and careful decision-making. Its slow pace also symbolized longevity and resilience.

Moreover, the tortoise's shell served as a symbol of protection and defense. Its ability to retreat into its shell when threatened represented the importance of self-preservation and the need for individuals to create boundaries and safeguards in their lives. This aspect of the tortoise's nature was often used as a metaphor for personal boundaries and self-care within the Luo community.

By nurturing a reverence for the tortoise, the Luo people demonstrated their deep understanding of the interconnectedness between humans and the natural world. The tortoise served as a reminder of the importance of living in harmony with nature and treating all living beings with respect and compassion.

Overall, the cultural significance of the tortoise in Luo society extended beyond its physical attributes. It represented important values such as respect for life, patience, protection, and the interconnectedness of generations. By instilling these beliefs and teachings in children, the Luo community sought to cultivate a sense of empathy, wisdom, and responsibility towards the natural world and their fellow human beings.

Monitor Lizard

In Luo culture, the monitor lizard, known as "ng'ech," held a special place of respect and value due to its beneficial role in the community. The monitor lizard's diet primarily consisted of black mambas, highly venomous snakes that posed a significant threat to humans and livestock. This natural predation by the monitor lizard made it a valuable asset in the eyes of the Luo people.

The presence of the monitor lizard in the environment was seen as a form of natural pest control, specifically for the black mamba population. Its ability to prey upon these dangerous snakes helped to reduce the risk of snakebite incidents and protect both human lives and livestock from the venomous threat. The monitor lizard's hunting abilities and preference for black mambas made it a valuable ally to the Luo community.

Due to its beneficial role in maintaining a balance in the ecosystem and providing a measure of safety, the monitor lizard was not harmed by the Luo people. They recognized the lizard's significance and purpose in the natural order of things and thus refrained from any actions that could harm or disturb it.

The respect for the monitor lizard extended beyond its practical contributions. It was also seen as a symbol of strength and resilience. The monitor lizard's scaly skin and robust appearance were associated with attributes such as tenacity, adaptability, and survival instincts. These characteristics were admired and respected by the Luo people, who often drew inspiration from the natural world around them.

Furthermore, the monitor lizard had cultural and spiritual connotations in Luo traditions. It was sometimes associated with ancestral beliefs and considered a spiritual messenger or symbol. Its appearance in certain contexts or locations was believed to carry symbolic messages or indicate the presence of ancestral spirits. As a result, the monitor lizard was regarded with reverence and treated with care to honor these spiritual connections.

By valuing and protecting the monitor lizard, the Luo people demonstrated their deep understanding of the intricate relationship between humans and the natural world. They recognized the importance of maintaining ecological balance and appreciating the contributions of different species, even those that might be seen as less conventionally attractive or appealing. The monitor lizard's role as a predator of black mambas served as a reminder of the interconnectedness of species and the benefits of coexistence.

Overall, the presence of the monitor lizard in Luo culture represented a harmonious relationship with nature, acknowledging the significance of its ecological role, and honoring the spiritual and cultural associations tied to this remarkable reptile.

Birds

Birds in the Lake Victoria region played diverse and significant roles in the lives of the local inhabitants. They were not only a source of food but also held cultural, traditional, and ecological importance. Here, we will explore the significance of two specific bird species: the Crested Crane and the Arum Tidi.

The Crested Crane, known as "gaali" in the local language, held special cultural and symbolic value among the Baganda people. It was not only conserved as their totem but also became a national symbol of peace and grace for Uganda. The Crested Crane's elegant appearance and graceful movements made it highly respected, and its conservation became a point of pride for Ugandans, particularly in their efforts to protect the vast wetlands where the bird is found. The conservation of wetlands in Uganda is recognized and appreciated throughout Africa, highlighting the country's commitment to environmental preservation.

Another important bird in the region was the Arum Tidi, a hornbill species. The Arum Tidi played a crucial role in the agricultural practices of the Luo community. It helped in checking the population of moles and mice that posed a threat to crops. The presence of the Arum Tidi in farmlands was welcomed and even encouraged by the elders, as it served as a natural pest control agent. By preying on these destructive rodents, the bird helped safeguard the farmers' livelihoods and ensured successful harvests.

Additionally, the Arum Tidi played a role in maintaining ecological balance by preying on dangerous snakes. Its ability to control snake populations contributed to the overall safety of the community, as snakes posed a significant risk to humans and livestock. The bird's natural inclination to hunt these venomous reptiles made it a valuable ally to the farmers and earned their respect.

However, despite the benefits associated with the Arum Tidi, there was also a certain level of fear and superstition surrounding the bird. If the Arum Tidi perched on someone's roof or hooted near their home, it was believed to be a foreboding sign of bad luck or an impending misfortune. This fear might have stemmed from the understanding that disturbing the natural balance of the ecosystem could have unintended consequences. By respecting and preserving the Arum Tidi, the community aimed to maintain harmony in nature and avoid any disruption to the delicate ecological equilibrium.

Various stories and folklore within the society emphasized the importance of not harming or killing the Arum Tidi. These tales likely served as a means of instilling respect and understanding of the bird's role in the community and the larger ecosystem. By nurturing a sense of reverence and taboo surrounding the bird's well-being, the community reinforced the significance of maintaining the delicate balance of nature and the interconnectedness of all living beings.

In conclusion, the birds of the Lake Victoria region, such as the Crested Crane and the Arum Tidi, played multifaceted roles in the lives of the local inhabitants. They were valued for their cultural symbolism, their contributions to agricultural practices, and their ecological significance. The conservation and respect for these birds reflected the communities' deep understanding of the importance of environmental stewardship and the interdependencies within the natural world.

Snakes

Snakes held diverse cultural significance among the Sukuma people, leading to certain cultural attachments and practices associated with these reptiles. While some snakes were revered and protected, others were utilized in traditional dances and even as medicinal resources.

Among the Sukuma people, there was a cultural understanding that certain snakes were not to be harmed. This reverence for snakes stemmed from their spiritual and symbolic associations within the community. Some snakes were believed to embody ancestral spirits or possess divine qualities and harming them would be seen as disrespectful or even sacrilegious. This cultural attachment and respect for snakes contributed to their conservation within Sukuma society.

Furthermore, snakes played a role in traditional dances performed by the Sukuma people. Dances such as "buzwilili," "hugoyangi," and "buyeye" incorporated snake imagery and movements, mimicking the serpentine nature of these creatures. The dances aimed to capture the essence and characteristics of snakes, infusing the performances with cultural and artistic significance. By incorporating snakes into their dances, the Sukuma people celebrated the inherent beauty and unique qualities of these reptiles.

In addition to their cultural roles, certain snakes were also used for medicinal purposes by traditional healers. These healers would utilize specific snake species in their healing practices, recognizing their potential therapeutic properties. The snakes would be carefully captured, killed, and prepared for medicinal use. Once killed, the snakes were dried and ground into a powder, which served as the final medicinal product. Traditional healers would administer this snake-derived medicine to treat various ailments and health conditions.

The use of snakes in traditional medicine reflects the Sukuma people's deep knowledge and understanding of the natural world. They recognized that certain snake species possessed medicinal properties and incorporated them into their healing practices. The utilization of snake-derived medicines highlights the Sukuma people's holistic approach to healthcare, acknowledging the potential healing powers found within nature.

In conclusion, snakes held cultural and medicinal significance among the Sukuma people. While certain snakes were revered and protected, others were incorporated into traditional dances or used as medicinal resources by traditional healers. The Sukuma people's cultural attachments to snakes and their utilization in various practices reflect their deep connection with nature and their understanding of the interplay between humans and the natural world.

Plate 11: A Tradotopma; Snake Dancing Ritual.

It should be observed that traditional healers, dancers, sorcerers/ sorceresses and traditional ritual performers took the lead in preserving snakes and other reptiles. They had undocumented rights to them because in case there was a snake troubling community members threes people would be called upon to catch it or kill it. Below are examples of snakes and their cultural functions.

Table 1: Indigenous names of snakes and reptiles

Indigenous names of snakes and reptiles	Cultural Functions
Sato (python)	Sign of peace to its beholders Its dropping is used as medicine Used in some traditional dances Its skin is used as part of cultural costumes during some ritual performance
Sawadi	Local dances/traditional dances Medicine and Threat to thieves
Ibambahili	Local dances/traditional dances Medicine and Threat to thieves
Kipili	Local dances/traditional dances Medicine and Threat to thieves

Nhagabuganga	Local dances/traditional dances Medicine and Threat to thieves
Kipalangoka	Local dances/traditional dances Medicine and Threat to thieves
Mvubi	Local dances/traditional dances Medicine and Threat to thieves
Ndolalimi	Local dances/traditional dances Medicine and Threat to thieves
Nkangakukwi	Local dances/traditional dances Medicine and Threat to thieves
Ludutu	Local dances/traditional dances Medicine and Threat to thieves
Mhela	Local dances/traditional dances Medicine and Local dances/traditional dances Medicine and Threat to thieves
Chambandinho	Local dances/traditional dances Medicine and Threat to thieves
Kabote	Local dances/traditional dances Medicine and Threat to thieves
Luhuhi	Local dances/traditional dances Medicine and Threat to thieves

Nzubi	Local dances/traditional dances
	Medicine and
	Threat to thieves
Masota	Local dances/traditional dances
	Medicine and
	Threat to thieves

Among the Luos and Suba communities, there was a cultural taboo against killing big snakes, and they held a special reverence for these creatures. Certain snake species, such as Nyangidi and Ngulusi, were highly respected and protected within their cultural beliefs.

In particular, the Luo people of Nyakach held the python, known as omieri, in great esteem. The omieri python was believed to be a reincarnation of one of their ancestors, carrying the ancestral spirit within it. This belief connected the snake to their lineage and heritage, emphasizing its sacred nature. As a result, it was strictly prohibited to harm or kill the omieri python or any other large snakes in the community.

Instead of harming these revered serpents, the Luos and Suba would provide them with offerings in the form of food, such as fowls and goats. This act of feeding the snakes symbolized their respect and acknowledgment of their ancestral connection. The belief was that by honoring these snakes, they would bring blessings and good fortune to the community. By treating the snakes with reverence, the people sought to maintain a harmonious relationship with the natural world and their ancestral spirits.

The cultural taboo against killing big snakes among the Luos and Suba reflected their deep spiritual and ancestral beliefs. It demonstrated their understanding of the interconnectedness between humans, nature, and the spirit world. By preserving and respecting these snakes, they upheld their cultural heritage and maintained a balance between the physical and spiritual realms.

Furthermore, the respect for big snakes in these communities was also tied to their ecological significance. Snakes, especially those found in the wetlands like the Ngulusi, played a vital role in maintaining the ecosystem's balance. They helped control populations of rodents and other small animals, thus preventing crop damage and potential disease transmission. Recognizing the ecological importance of these snakes, the communities embraced their presence and protected them as part of their environmental stewardship.

In conclusion, the Luo and Suba communities held a deep respect for big snakes, considering them as manifestations of their ancestors and bringers of good fortune. The cultural taboo against killing these snakes, such as the revered omieri python, reflected their spiritual beliefs and ancestral connections. By providing offerings and treating these snakes with respect, the communities sought to maintain a harmonious relationship with the natural world and uphold their cultural heritage. Additionally, their reverence for these snakes also acknowledged their ecological significance in preserving the balance of the wetland ecosystems they inhabited.

Plate 12: Snake Charmer at Bujora, Tanzania

Chapter 8
Traditional Technology

The Role of Traditional Technology in Natural Resource Management

Traditional technology played a significant role in natural resource management, particularly in terms of environmental friendliness and the conservation of natural resources. Unlike modern technology, traditional practices often had minimal or no negative impact on the environment, ensuring the sustainability of resources.

One example of traditional technology's effectiveness can be seen in Hayaland, where legumes like beans and bambara nuts were preserved using a mixture of ash. This practice effectively controlled the attack of pests such as sytophillus sp., reducing the need for chemical pesticides. Similarly, the use of ash mixed with ground tobacco leaves as a rub on the cow's skin helped control ticks in cattle without resorting to chemical treatments. In the case of coffee, a fungal disease was treated by applying hippopotamus dung to the leaves, offering a natural remedy. Coffee husks were also burned as a control measure against the disease.

Despite the advantages of traditional technology, it has been overshadowed by modern technology, which is often seen as more superior and aligned with the demands of the modern world. While there is some truth to this perspective, there are still proponents who believe that traditional technology can complement modern approaches. It is important to note that with the process of modernization, the introduction of new species of pests and diseases has made some traditional techniques less effective.

For instance, cereal weevils (escania) no longer respond easily to the traditional method of mixing beans with ash, making it necessary to explore alternative control methods, including chemical interventions.

On the other hand, the use of modern technology in natural resource management has revealed several negative effects. For example, the constant use of inorganic fertilizers can make the soil heavily reliant on these inputs, making it challenging to achieve good harvests without their application. Farmers have also reported that the use of chemicals in cow dips for tick control resulted in the unintended consequences of killing various bird species. These birds play a crucial role in the biological control of ticks, highlighting the unintended ecological consequences of certain modern practices.

Balancing the advantages and disadvantages of traditional and modern technology is crucial for sustainable natural resource management. Recognizing the value of traditional practices and integrating them with appropriate modern technologies can potentially lead to more environmentally friendly and sustainable approaches that address the challenges of resource conservation in a rapidly changing world.

Traditional Tools

Sukuma people applied different tools and instruments in carrying out various activities related to their livelihood. Their tools and instruments permitted natural rate of multiplication and sustainable development of these resources.

Hand-Hoes: Before iron works reached Sukumaland people dug their fields with hoes made of mahogany wood, locally called gembe. These hoes, therefore, were also called "magembe".

Rongo people endowed with iron hoes to Sukumaland. They also lorged hoes and other iron tools after settling at some places within Sukumaland. Three major types of doffing implements were manufactured, namely, igembe (hoe), lucholonga nad ngogotejo.

Traditional tools played a crucial role in the daily lives of the Sukuma people, enabling them to carry out various activities related to their livelihoods. These tools were designed to promote the natural rate of multiplication and sustainable development of resources.

One of the primary tools used by the Sukuma people was the hand-hoe. Before the introduction of iron tools to Sukumaland, people relied on hoes made from mahogany wood, known locally as "gembe." These wooden hoes, commonly referred to as "magembe," were instrumental in cultivating the land and preparing fields for planting. They allowed farmers to loosen the soil and remove weeds, ensuring the successful growth of crops.

The introduction of iron hoes by the Rongo people had a significant impact on agriculture in Sukumaland. The Rongo settlers brought iron hoes and other iron tools with them, which gradually replaced the wooden hoes. These iron hoes were more durable and efficient, making farming tasks easier and more productive.

Among the iron implements produced by the Sukuma people, three major types of digging tools were prominent. The first was the "igembe," which refers to the iron hoe. This hoe had a sturdy iron blade attached to a wooden handle, providing a more effective tool for digging and cultivating the soil.

The second type of digging implement was the "lucholonga," which was a large iron shovel-like tool used for digging deeper holes or trenches. It was particularly useful for tasks such as constructing irrigation channels or digging wells.

The third type was the "ngogotejo," which was a smaller iron hoe used for more delicate tasks like weeding and cultivating smaller areas of land. Its compact size and sharp blade allowed for precise and efficient work, promoting the healthy growth of crops.

These traditional tools not only facilitated agricultural activities but also played a role in other aspects of Sukuma life, such as construction and craftsmanship. For instance, the wooden hoes made from mahogany wood could be used for shaping and smoothing wooden beams or planks in construction projects.

Overall, the use of traditional tools by the Sukuma people exemplified their sustainable approach to resource management.

By utilizing these tools, they were able to work the land and engage in various activities while preserving the natural environment and promoting the long-term sustainability of their resources.

Plate 13: A traditional Blacksmith

The advantages of these doffing tools, as far as land and soil conservation is concerned, are first, peasants could not dig the land/soil up to loosen it and therefore expose it more to both physical and chemical erosion agents. Second, peasants using it would not cultivate big farms because the tools themselves were not that efficient. Third, cultivation under the existing technology did not encourage commercial farming that usually lead to over-cultivation and hence soil/land overuse.

The Abayesi clan made hand-hoes from locally available iron. They specialized in iron mongering. They made handles from locally available iron. Hoes made of iron were called amahaha. Another type of hoe made of iron was called olubale made from one type of iron known as engedezyo.

Colonial governments forbade indigenous ironsmiths from manufacturing hand-hoes and other iron products. Instead, they encouraged foreigners to do so. This is why in 1922 a Greek opened a hand-hoe factory for the first time on this island. The advantage of a hand-hoe as related to soil or land conservation is that, while using it. It is not easy to plough the soil so deep as to expose it to the risks of soil erosion.

Hunting Tools: Hunters used bows and arrows, clubs, hunting dogs, nets made of sisal fibres, trapping holes and kraals. Obviously, these tools were not devastating for they had limited and specific catching capacities. The introduction of guns resulted in the extermination of large number of wildlife resources

Metal Tools: The Bahaya people as well as the whole region of Kagera commony used various tools, which were smelt from iron ore, obtained from parts of Kiziba and Itahwa. For example they used homemade spears for hunting and protecting themselves against intruders. The blacksmiths made different types of hoes for different functions. The craftsmen used large "eyeless" needless or spikes for making baskets. A special tool was designed for digging banana plantation and trimming the banana leaves. Generally, the Bahaya were very proud of their locally manufactured tools.

Chapter 9
Cultural Sites

The Kagera region is rich in cultural sites that hold significant historical and traditional value. Among these sites are Kyaya, Bunikangomea in Kahororo ward, and Rwamishenye Division, each with its unique story and importance.

Kyaya, known for its special type of soil called "ironi," holds a particular significance in the enthronement of chiefs. According to legend, long ago, during the enthronement process, "inoni" was smeared on the face of the chief. A person stood by, listening attentively to determine if the chief would sniff or not. Sniffing meant that the chief was not fit for the throne, and the entire process had to be repeated. Originally, "inoni" was used only for chiefs of Maruka and Kiziba, but it later became customary for Kyamtwara and Bugabo chiefs as well. This "inoni" possesses a miraculous quality, shifting from one place to another. Sometimes it can be found on the ground, while at other times, it can be seen spread over the surface of the lake, resembling ash.

In Bunukangomea, a sub-village within the region, there is a notable artifact called "enyondo." This heavy hammer is accompanied by other accessories such as a smelt hoe, a knife, and a "panga." It is believed that "enyondo" has been present in Bunukangomea for the past 17 generations. It was brought by Rugomota Owolugundu, a man who originated from Uganda. Rugomota Owolugundu traveled through various places in Bukoba District, naming them along the way. Upon reaching the sub-village of Bunukangomea, he decided to leave "enyondo" and its accompanying accessories there. He eventually settled in Maruku, where he established a kingdom. The "enyondo" could be lifted from its place, but once lifted, it could not be removed from the ground without certain rituals being performed at the site.

The Kerewe people, on the other hand, constructed caves on hills as a means of self-protection against invasions and for safeguarding items of cultural and social importance. These caves, still in relatively good condition, serve as a testament to the ancient practices and customs of the Kerewe chiefs. Additionally, the region is home to other significant sites, including chief's graveyards, locations for traditional rituals, and remarkable geographical features.

These cultural sites not only serve as historical landmarks but also embody the rich heritage and traditions of the local communities. They provide a glimpse into the past, preserving the customs and beliefs that have shaped the identity of the Kagera region. It is crucial to recognize, respect, and protect these sites to ensure that future generations can continue to appreciate and learn from the cultural heritage they represent.

Table 2: Character, Location and Cultural Value of the Sukuma.

Character / site	Location	Cultural value	Person/ Clan Concerned
Nabuta Cave	East of Nansio metresChief's security	Chief's security	
Kiregi cave	Kiregi Island	Chief's security	
Handebezyo	Halwego	German Stronghold and First Catholic Missionaries Settlement	

Makiyanga Cave	Busangani	Chief's security	
Malelema Cave	Malelema	Chief's security	
Kalage Ka Buha	Saku	Magic Performance	
Chief Katobaha's foot Island	Kamasi	Chief Katobaha's foot marks	
Chiefs' yard – grave (Kitare)	Buhwi	Chiefs' yard grave	
Chief's tomb	Buzunzya	Chief's tomb	
The oldest Bana Island plant century	Kumasi	A banana Plant, planted in the 6th century, still alive	
Ngoma hill Island	Buluzya	Traditional and cultural ritual still practiced (no longer allowed)	Ababwalumi
Bukunu	Irugwa	Traditional and cultural ritual still practiced (no dog allowed)	Ababwalumi
Nsenga	Kulazu Island	Traditional and cultural rituals still practiced	

Kweru A	Kweru	Cultural ritual still practiced	Abasegena
Mikuyu Ya Basegana	Busegena	Cultural ritual still practiced	Abasegena
Malisasili District	Maliasili	Cultural ritual still practiced	Abasegena
Rugezi	Rugezi (Ferry) Nankala	Cultural rituals still practiced	Abayango
Nambuye Island	Nambuye	Cultural rituals still practiced	Abalimbuka and Abakula
Ebulongo (A Mlima Marvelous Tree)	Nyamango		
Ngoma ya Mubule	Mubule	Cultural rituals still practiced	
Wasilanga Chiefdom Headquarters	Kamasi Island Chiefdom Headquarters		
Kahumilo Cave	200 metres south of Nabuta	Chief's security	
Kwaya Cave	Bukwya	Chief's security and signs	

Source: S. Majeng, for this study

During the period between 1500 AD and 1760 A.D. many tribes from many directions invaded. Sukumaland as it is known today. Through intermarriage, cultural mixing economic nad commercial relations and lack of a common language they formed Sukuma tribe with Sukuma as their language that united them.

The Luo and Abasuba of Kenya had very many legendry/cultural sites. These were places of significant historical phenomenon or mythical incidents. Sometimes, they were places of a legendary fame or ritualistic functions. Whatever the case may be these places were and some are sill held in awe and fear reinforced by traditional teachings of the tribes. There are sites, which in one way or another, affected or contributed greatly to the lives of people in the community. They were sites where various meetings and practices such as sacrifices, rainmaking, and cleansing took or are still taking place. For example, Simbi Nyaima, Nyamgondho, Lwanda Magere, Kit Mikati, Thim Lye Lich Ohinga, the islands such as Atego, Ringiti, Mbasa na Muole, Nyama ni Ware and many others.

Kit Mikayi

Kit Mikayi, also known as "the stone of the first wife," is a renowned cultural site located in Seme Location, Kisumu District, Kenya. The site is associated with a captivating legend that has been passed down through generations.

According to the legend, an old man deeply loved a woman, but unfortunately, after being married for about ten years, they had only been blessed with one child. One day, the woman returned from her motherland carrying a mail (kapid) with her. Upon seeing this, the old man made the decision to take her as his second wife. To the old man's delight, the younger wife bore him numerous children. However, this sudden abundance of children ignited jealousy and animosity within the heart of the first wife.

As a result, the family was consumed by incessant wrangling and fights, causing discord and unrest. Witnessing the endless feuds and the unhappiness they brought, God decided to intervene. In an act of divine intervention, God transformed the family members into stones, forever freezing them in their quarrelsome state.

The myth surrounding Kit Mikayi serves as a poignant reminder that God does not look favorably upon those who remain discontented with their blessings. It acts as a public censure of the disgruntled and serves to caution individuals against harboring jealousy and animosity towards others. The story carries a moral lesson, emphasizing the importance of gratitude and contentment.

Kit Mikayi holds a special significance for barren women who visit the site with hopes of receiving the gift of fertility and children. These women offer sacrifices at the site, seeking blessings and divine intervention in their desire to conceive. The cultural belief associated with Kit Mikayi instills faith and hope in the hearts of those who visit, fostering a sense of connection to the spiritual realm and the power it holds.

The site itself is revered and held in awe by the local community. Its environment has been conserved meticulously over the years, preserving its natural beauty and cultural sanctity. Kit Mikayi stands as a testament to the enduring traditions and beliefs of the Luo people, reminding them of the importance of gratitude, harmony, and the power of the divine in their lives.

Plate 14: Kit Mikayi in Seme, Kisumu.

Atego Hill (Got)

Atego Hill, also known as Got, is a remarkable phenomenon that emerged in Mfangano Island, located in Lake Victoria. Its appearance and the surrounding legend are intriguing and have contributed to its status as a revered cultural and conservation site.

The story of Atego Hill began with a dream that appeared to the people of Masisi, a community on Mfangano Island. The dream conveyed a request for the people to allow the hill to reside among them. However, when the people initially rejected the request, the hill mysteriously disappeared. Later on, it reappeared in Wasamo, another region of the island, and brought forth another dream. This time, the Wasamo clan agreed to welcome and accommodate the hill, allowing it to stay.

The emergence of Atego Hill and its connection to dreams and visions have imbued it with a sense of mystical significance. The communities residing in its vicinity hold deep respect for the hill and its spiritual presence. Consequently, there are strict cultural traditions and beliefs that govern the interaction with the hill.

Due to its legendary appearance and the belief in its spiritual essence, the communities surrounding Atego Hill refrain from landing their boats on its shores or cutting trees from the area. The hill is treated as a sacred site and is primarily conserved for the growth of medicinal plants. This conservation effort ensures that the natural flora and fauna in the vicinity of Atego Hill are protected and preserved.

The Kenyan side of Lake Victoria is home to several islands that possess similar legendary stories and cultural significance. Some of these islands are inhabited solely by wild goats and sheep, adding to their mystique and allure. The legends and traditions associated with these islands have contributed to their conservation and the protection of their unique ecosystems.

Atego Hill, along with other islands and cultural sites in the Lake Victoria region, serves as a testament to the deep-rooted beliefs, folklore, and respect for nature among the local communities. These sites not only hold historical and mythical value but also contribute to the conservation of biodiversity and the preservation of traditional cultural practices. They serve as reminders of the interconnectedness between humans and the natural world, fostering a sense of harmony and reverence for the environment.

Nyamgodho wuod (son of) Ombare

The tale of Nyamgodho wuod Ombare, the son of Ombare, is a captivating legend from the shores of Lake Victoria. Nyamgodho was a humble fisherman who lived in poverty, relying on the lake for his livelihood. One fateful day, he encountered an elderly woman in the waters of the lake and, overcoming his initial fear, he rescued her and brought her to his home.

As time went on, Nyamgodho and the lake woman developed a deep bond and eventually got married. With her presence, the household experienced a sudden transformation as wealth and prosperity flowed into their lives. However, Nyamgodho's newfound success led to arrogance and a change in his behavior. He started mistreating the lake woman, forgetting the kindness she had shown him.

Unable to bear the mistreatment any longer, the lake woman made a fateful decision. She returned to the lake, and astonishingly, everything in Nyamgodho's home, including the domestic animals, children, and other wives, followed her into the depths of the water. Nyamgodho, filled with remorse and desperation, pleaded and cried out, but his pleas went unanswered. As everything vanished into the lake, he himself transformed into a massive stone, forever commemorating his tragic fate.

The legend of Nyamgodho wuod Ombare lives on, and it is said that the footprints of the lake woman and her retinue can still be seen in Nyandwa, a place located in the Gwassi Division of Suba District. This enduring tale serves as a cautionary reminder about the consequences of arrogance and mistreatment, emphasizing the importance of gratitude, kindness, and respect.

The presence of the footprints in Nyandwa is regarded with reverence and awe, becoming a site of cultural significance. It serves as a symbol of the lake woman's power and the consequences that befell Nyamgodho. The footprints and the accompanying legend contribute to the preservation of the cultural heritage of the community and serve as a reminder of the interplay between human actions, consequences, and the mystical forces believed to inhabit the lake.

Data Kibaye (King) and Witewe

Data Kibaye and Witewe were two brothers from the Abakunta tribe in Buganda who, due to committing a grave offense, were forced to flee their homeland. Seeking refuge, they found themselves in Suba land, specifically in the region of Gwassi. Gwassi became their new home, and it was there that they encountered the Ongo people who had previously left Buganda.

The descendants of Data Kibaye and Witewe, who now reside in various locations within Gwassi, have become known as traditional conservationists due to their strong cultural beliefs and practices regarding nature. These beliefs have been passed down through generations, shaping their interactions with the environment and reinforcing the importance of conservation.

One notable example of their commitment to cultural preservation and conservation is the conservation of the Gwassi hills. These hills hold great significance in their cultural practices and are protected as sacred sites. The local communities have actively worked to preserve the natural beauty and integrity of the hills, recognizing their importance within their cultural heritage.

Beyond Gwassi, cultural and historical sites in Uganda also contribute to the preservation and celebration of their cultural heritage. The Kabaka Tombs serve as a burial ground for the kings of Buganda, showcasing the rich history and traditions of the region. Namirembe Cathedral, one of the oldest and most significant Anglican cathedrals in Uganda, holds religious and cultural importance for the community.

The Uganda Martyrs, a group of Christian converts who were martyred for their faith, are remembered and honored at various sites across the country. Owen Falls (now known as Nalubaale Dam) holds significance as a hydroelectric power station and a landmark at the source of the River Nile. Budhaghali, also located at the source of the Nile, is a sacred place where rituals and ceremonies take place.

These cultural sites in Uganda serve as reminders of the country's history, traditions, and the importance of preserving and celebrating cultural heritage. They attract visitors and locals alike, offering insights into the diverse cultural fabric of the region and contributing to the collective identity of the people. By valuing and conserving these sites, communities are able to maintain a strong connection to their past while fostering cultural continuity for future generations.

Chapter 10
Gender and Religion in Conservation

The Role and Effect of Gender in Conservation

In the Sukuma culture, both men and women played vital roles in land conservation and agriculture. The division of labor between genders was structured based on their strengths, responsibilities, and traditional practices. Men primarily focused on clearing and preparing the land for cultivation, including the planting of trees and other vegetation species that served as conservation measures. Their involvement in these activities aimed to maintain soil fertility, prevent erosion, and create a sustainable agricultural ecosystem.

On the other hand, women took on the responsibilities of collecting food crops and processing them into consumable meals. Their expertise and knowledge were crucial in transforming harvested crops into nourishing food for the community. For instance, the thrashing of millet and sorghum, which required physical strength, was typically undertaken by men. In contrast, women in the Sukuma culture were actively involved in various stages of food processing, including pounding grains, grinding flour, and cooking meals. They held invaluable knowledge of traditional food preparation methods and recipes that had been passed down through generations.

It is important to note that the division of labor and gender roles may differ among different ethnic groups within the Lake Victoria region. For example, the Luo community, unlike the Sukuma, may have had different gender-specific responsibilities and practices. In the Luo culture, women might have been primarily responsible for all household duties, including agriculture, food production, and processing, reflecting their unique cultural traditions and societal dynamics.

In the Sukuma culture, the agricultural practices were closely aligned with the lunar calendar, which guided their food production schedule. The Sukuma people had a deep understanding of the lunar cycles, and they knew which activities were suitable for each month. With a year consisting of 354 days, the Sukuma community had developed a synchronized system of agricultural practices that maximized their harvests and ensured sustainable food production.

The significance of gender in conservation and agriculture extends beyond the specific roles individuals played. Gender dynamics influence decision-making processes, resource management, and the overall effectiveness of conservation efforts. Recognizing and empowering both men and women as key stakeholders in conservation initiatives can lead to more inclusive and sustainable outcomes.

Promoting gender equality in conservation involves providing equal access to resources, education, and opportunities for both men and women. It requires fostering an environment that values and respects the diverse perspectives, skills, and knowledge that each gender brings to the table. By involving women in decision-making processes, their unique insights and experiences can contribute to more holistic and effective conservation strategies. Furthermore, empowering women economically and socially can enhance their capacity to engage in sustainable practices and influence positive change within their communities.

In conclusion, gender roles and dynamics have influenced traditional agricultural practices and conservation efforts in the Lake Victoria region. Understanding and acknowledging these gender-specific roles and contributions are essential for implementing inclusive and sustainable conservation initiatives. By recognizing the value of both men and women in conservation, we can work towards creating a more equitable and resilient future for both the natural environment and the communities that depend on it.

Sukuma people had their own food-production schedule.

They knew what to do during one or the other moon (month). A Sukuma year had 354 days.

Table 3: Sukuma Year and Cultivation/Farming Schedule

Sukuma Month	Calendar Year	Season	Activity	Weather
Lubingo	November	Rain season	Cultivation Begins	Some rains
Mili	December	Rain Season	Weed clearing and stalk collection for ridge making	Some rains
Satu	January	Rain season	Preparation of buds for paddy	Rainy and sunny
Nne	February	Rain season	Weeding	Rainy and sunny
Sano	March	Rain season	Crops ripen	Heavy rains
Ntandatu	April	Rain season	Crops ripen, paddy buds are full of water	Heavy rains
Mpungati	May	Rain season	Second weeding, harvesting begins	Heavy rains
Nane	June	Dry season sets in	Harvesting continues, house construction	Dry season and no rains
Nkenda	July	Dry season	Cotton sorting and cotton selling, Building construction	Dry season and humid

Nkumi	August	Dry season	Cotton selling/buying continues (people have money now for construction	Dry season
Lyambalwa/ Lyana Iya Nkumi/ Kinyela Mbeho	September	Dry season	Construction, traditional dances begin	Dry season, windy and hot
Igabanha/ Lizukulu Iya Nkumi	October	Dry season	Land reallocation (if any) Traditional dances	Partly dry and partly wet

Such a schedule was followed strictly and in a way sided to the conservation of soil. Women collected firewood from dead dry plants and males went into forests fro house building materials kuzingula and for other activities such as hunting, herbs and honey collection. Males had to construct houses for that households. Both females and males knew exactly what plant species were used for the purpose. They knew what trees were untouchable except in specific cases and cultural functions.

By and large, males went fishing, preserved forests for cultural rituals, dug and maintained well for drinking water and protected pasture and grazing land for their livestock. Males made appropriate fishing equipment to ensure that only the right fish were caught and sparingly. Children, males and females participated in what adults were doing.

The Role and Effect of Religion

The arrival of Christian missionaries, specifically Catholic priests, in Sukuma land in the late 19th century had a profound impact on the religious and cultural landscape of the region. The missionaries sought to spread the Word of God and establish a Christian presence among the Sukuma people. In 1878, the first missionaries passed through Sukuma land on their way to Uganda, and four years later, in 1882, they returned and requested permission from Chief Kiganga of Bukumbi to settle in the area. The chief agreed, and a covenant of everlasting friendship and brotherhood was made between the Catholic priests and the Bakumbi people of Bukumbi. To solemnize this agreement, they engaged in a symbolic ritual of drinking one another's blood, symbolizing their deep commitment to their newfound relationship.

With the establishment of Catholic missions, the priests began teaching the Sukuma people about Christianity and administering the sacrament of baptism. This meant that those who converted to Christianity were expected to embrace the teachings of the Catholic Church and distance themselves from their traditional and cultural religious practices. Traditional dances and the role of traditional herbalists were discouraged, and these cultural and spiritual attachments were often labeled as devilish or pagan. As a result, converts began to lose their connection and respect for culturally revered animals and trees, which had played a significant role in the conservation and preservation of natural resources within their environment.

The missionaries introduced new elements to the Sukuma landscape, such as exotic trees and flowers, which captured the attention of the converts. The construction of parishes and schools in Sukumaland also brought in school bands and foreign games like football, replacing local and traditional dances and games. The emphasis on foreign activities further discouraged schoolboys and girls from participating in their own cultural practices, including those related to the conservation of natural resources. This shift in focus and values meant that the cultural respect for and practices of conserving natural resources, which had been deeply rooted in Sukuma traditions, were at risk of being neglected and forgotten by the converts.

The introduction of Christianity and the associated changes in religious practices and cultural values had a significant impact on the Sukuma people's relationship with their environment. The traditional wisdom and practices that had guided sustainable resource management for generations were gradually eroded, replaced by foreign ideologies and practices that did not prioritize the conservation of fauna and flora based on cultural and traditional beliefs. This transformation underscored the complex interplay between religion, culture, and conservation, highlighting the need for a nuanced understanding and appreciation of the diverse factors that influence human interactions with the natural world.

It is important to note that while the influence of Christianity and the associated changes had certain negative effects on traditional conservation practices, they also brought positive aspects, such as the introduction of formal education and new agricultural techniques that could have contributed to increased productivity and improved livelihoods for some Sukuma individuals. The overall impact on conservation efforts, however, necessitates a balanced approach that recognizes the importance of cultural heritage and traditional ecological knowledge while incorporating sustainable practices that align with evolving societal needs and values.

Chapter 11
Endangered Animal, Plant, and Insect Species

This chapter explores the plight of endangered animal, plant, and insect species in the Lake Victoria region. The "red list" serves as a valuable tool for assessing the diversity and condition of the ecosystem in this area. By identifying and highlighting threatened individual species, the red list forms the foundation for developing sustainable strategies and conservation measures to protect these vulnerable organisms.

Threatened Plant Species

The vulnerability of threatened plant species in the Lake Victoria region demands urgent attention and conservation efforts. While a comprehensive evaluation of the region's flora is lacking, insights from the Luo community have provided valuable information regarding specific endangered species. Among them, the ng'ou (fig tree), ong'ora, Keya, and achak have been identified as particularly at risk.

The fig tree holds immense cultural and ecological significance for the Luo community. It has been a gathering point, offering shade for communal meetings and ceremonies. It has also served as a sacred site for worship, symbolizing the connection between nature and spirituality. The fig tree's branches and foliage have provided a habitat for a diverse range of birds and insects, contributing to the overall biodiversity of the area. The fruits of the fig tree have been an important source of sustenance, not only for humans but also for birds and fish, highlighting the interconnectedness of species in the ecosystem.

Traditional fishers, especially those who employ traditional fishing baskets, have long recognized the fig tree as a natural indicator of the presence of water underground. Its presence has guided them to select strategic locations for fishing, ensuring successful catches. However, the distribution of the fig tree has significantly declined in various places, such as Mfang'ano Island, Kiwa Island, and Muhuru Bay. The loss of these trees has not only impacted the ecological balance but has also eroded the cultural and traditional practices associated with them.

To address this concerning trend, concerted efforts are necessary to conserve the remaining fig trees and initiate reforestation projects along the shores of Lake Victoria. Conservation organizations, local communities, and policymakers must collaborate to raise awareness about the importance of these threatened plant species and implement strategies to safeguard their habitats. By promoting the planting and protection of fig trees, not only can we preserve the cultural heritage of the Luo community, but we can also maintain the ecological integrity of the region and support the interconnected web of life that depends on these trees.

Education and community involvement are crucial aspects of any conservation effort. Engaging local communities, especially the Luo community, in conservation initiatives can help foster a sense of ownership and pride in protecting their natural heritage. This can be achieved through awareness campaigns, workshops, and training programs that highlight the significance of these threatened plant species and the role they play in sustaining the local ecosystem.

Furthermore, collaboration between scientists, researchers, and traditional knowledge holders can enhance our understanding of these endangered plants and their ecological roles. By combining scientific knowledge with traditional ecological knowledge, we can develop comprehensive conservation strategies that consider both the scientific and cultural dimensions of these plant species.

In conclusion, the preservation of threatened plant species in the Lake Victoria region, including the ng'ou (fig tree) and others, requires immediate attention and action. By recognizing their cultural and ecological significance, promoting reforestation efforts, and engaging local communities, we can contribute to the conservation and restoration of the region's rich biodiversity. Through these collective efforts, we can ensure a sustainable future where these plants thrive, benefiting both the ecosystem and the communities that depend on them.

Threatened Birds

The avian inhabitants of the Lake Victoria region have always been a captivating sight, attracting bird enthusiasts and researchers from around the world. The region boasts a remarkable variety of bird species, including both terrestrial and aquatic birds. However, the rapid growth of human populations in the area has placed immense pressure on their habitats, leading to significant challenges for bird conservation.

As human settlements expanded and economic activities intensified, the natural habitats of many bird species suffered from degradation and fragmentation. This forced several terrestrial bird species to seek refuge in more remote areas, farther away from the Lake Basin. These birds, once a common sight near human settlements, now find themselves struggling to adapt to new environments that may not provide the same resources and conditions they rely upon.

Among the bird species closely tied to the lake ecosystem, the osou (Cormorants) have faced particular threats to their survival. These elegant waterbirds have traditionally thrived in the Lake Victoria region, relying on its abundant fish populations for sustenance. However, the destruction of their habitats has had severe consequences for their populations. One striking example is the decline of Cormorants on the Migingo Islands.

Not long ago, the Migingo Islands were a bustling sanctuary for these aquatic birds. Their large population was evident from the whitish droppings that adorned the islands, serving as a visual testimony to their presence. The islands were virtually uninhabited by humans, allowing the Cormorants to flourish undisturbed. Sadly, the arrival of migrant fishermen and the subsequent destruction of the islands' habitat have led to a dramatic decline in the Cormorant population. These magnificent birds, once a thriving community, now face the risk of near extinction in the area.

The decline of Cormorants is not only a loss in terms of biodiversity but also has broader ecological implications. Cormorants play a vital role in maintaining the balance of the aquatic ecosystem by regulating fish populations. Their decline disrupts the delicate equilibrium, potentially causing cascading effects throughout the food chain.

To address the challenges faced by threatened bird species, including the Cormorants, comprehensive conservation measures are essential. These efforts should encompass a combination of habitat restoration, targeted conservation programs, and strict regulations to protect their nesting and breeding grounds. Collaborative initiatives involving local communities, conservation organizations, and governmental agencies can help raise awareness about the importance of bird conservation and establish sustainable practices for the long-term protection of their habitats.

Furthermore, education and public outreach play a critical role in bird conservation. Engaging local communities, schools, and tourists in birdwatching activities, ecological awareness campaigns, and educational programs can foster a sense of appreciation and responsibility towards avian biodiversity. By highlighting the intrinsic value and ecological contributions of threatened bird species, we can inspire individuals and communities to become stewards of their natural environment.

Scientific research is also vital for understanding the specific needs and requirements of threatened bird species. By studying their behaviors, migratory patterns, and habitat preferences, researchers can provide valuable insights for conservation strategies. Furthermore, combining scientific knowledge with traditional ecological knowledge from local communities can lead to more comprehensive and culturally sensitive conservation approaches.

In conclusion, the decline of threatened bird species in the Lake

Victoria region, such as the Cormorants, necessitates immediate action to protect their habitats and restore their populations. By addressing the root causes of habitat destruction, implementing conservation programs, and raising awareness among local communities, we can work towards ensuring the long-term survival and well-being of these magnificent birds. Through collective efforts, we can safeguard their presence for future generations and maintain the ecological balance of the Lake Victoria ecosystem.

Threatened Animals

The Lake Victoria basin has a rich history of coexistence between humans and diverse animal species, both big and small. The region's beaches especially those in Luo Land, adorned with unique names, carry stories of the past, hinting at the animals that once thrived in these areas. One such beach is Luanda Magwar, which translates to "the rocks of zebra," evoking images of these majestic striped creatures roaming freely in their natural habitat. Another beach known as Wath Ong'er, meaning "the beach of monkeys," signifies the lively presence of playful primates in the region.

In the bygone era, the Lake Victoria basin was teeming with various big game species, each having their own designated watering points along the lake's shores. The elephants, with their remarkable memory and social bonds, were known to frequent specific locations where they quenched their thirst. However, legends tell a cautionary tale through the story of Maguma in Gwassi Location. Maguma's transgression, the unlawful killing of a young elephant, carried severe consequences. The spirits of the land deemed his actions taboo, resulting in his descent into madness and eventual demise. The repercussions of this incident reached beyond Maguma himself, as the elephants were compelled to seek refuge elsewhere, ultimately migrating to the renowned Maasai Mara.

While the migration of elephants altered the landscape and dynamics of the Lake Victoria basin, other species managed to adapt and endure. Among them, the buffalo, a resilient and formidable creature, continues to thrive in Labwe Village near Lake Victoria. These majestic herbivores, with their imposing presence and cooperative behavior within their herds, remind us of the enduring connection between the animal kingdom and the surrounding communities.

However, the conservation of threatened animal species remains a pressing concern in the Lake Victoria region. The survival of these animals depends on the preservation and restoration of their natural habitats, as well as the implementation of effective wildlife protection measures. This requires collaborative efforts between local communities, conservation organizations, and governmental agencies.

Conservation initiatives must prioritize the identification and protection of critical habitats and migration corridors that are crucial for the survival and well-being of threatened animal species. Additionally, community-based conservation programs can play a vital role in engaging and empowering local residents as custodians of the land. By involving communities in conservation activities, such as sustainable tourism, wildlife monitoring, and education, we can foster a sense of pride and responsibility for the region's unique biodiversity.

Moreover, scientific research plays a pivotal role in understanding the behavior, ecology, and conservation needs of threatened animal species. By studying their movements, habitat requirements, and population dynamics, scientists can provide valuable insights to guide conservation strategies. Collaborating with local communities and incorporating traditional ecological knowledge further enriches these efforts, as indigenous wisdom often holds valuable information about animal behavior and habitat utilization.

Preserving the balance between humans and wildlife in the Lake Victoria basin is crucial for maintaining a healthy and thriving ecosystem. Protecting the remaining populations of threatened animal species, such as elephants and other game species, not only ensures their survival but also contributes to the preservation of biodiversity and the overall well-being of the region.

In conclusion, the Lake Victoria basin's history is interwoven with the presence of diverse animal species, both past and present. While some species have faced challenges and migration due to human activities, others continue to persist, representing the resilience of nature. Efforts to safeguard threatened animal species require collaborative conservation approaches, incorporating scientific research, traditional knowledge, and community participation. By nurturing this harmonious coexistence, we can protect the animals that define the region's identity and maintain the ecological integrity of the Lake Victoria basin for generations to come.

Conclusion

The Lake Victoria region is grappling with the challenges of endangered animal, plant, and insect species. The diminishing populations and habitats of these organisms pose a threat to the region's biodiversity and ecological balance. Efforts are needed to conserve and protect the remaining plant species like the fig tree, as well as address the destruction of bird habitats and the decline of large game populations. Collaborative initiatives involving local communities, conservation organizations, and policymakers are essential to safeguarding these threatened species and restoring ecological

Chapter 12

Language's Integral Role in the Conservation of Natural Resources

Language is a fundamental element in promoting conservation efforts around the Lake Victoria region. It has been instrumental in raising awareness, facilitating policy formulation, preserving traditional knowledge, encouraging community participation, and enabling effective monitoring and evaluation. In this chapter, we will explore the various ways in which language has contributed to the conservation of resources in the area.

Language for Raising Awareness

Local languages have been crucial in creating awareness among the communities residing near Lake Victoria about the significance of conserving natural resources. Public campaigns, workshops, and radio shows conducted in local languages have played a vital role in educating people about sustainable practices like reforestation and proper waste disposal. By utilizing language as a means of communication, these initiatives have successfully disseminated knowledge and fostered a sense of responsibility toward resource conservation.

Language in Policy Formulation for Effective Conservation

Language plays a crucial role in policy formulation for conservation efforts in the Lake Victoria region. In this chapter, we delve into the significance of using local languages in policy development to ensure the effectiveness and success of conservation policies. By employing local languages, policymakers can bridge communication gaps, enhance understanding, and foster community engagement in conservation initiatives.

Enhancing Accessibility and Understanding

Conservation policies need to be accessible and understandable to the local communities who are directly impacted by them. By utilizing local languages, policymakers can break down language barriers and ensure that policies are effectively communicated. Translating policies into languages such as Luo, Luhya, and Kiswahili allows community members to comprehend the content, requirements, and objectives of the policies. This linguistic accessibility empowers individuals to actively participate in conservation efforts.

Promoting Inclusivity and Empowerment

Inclusive policymaking is essential to ensure that the diverse voices and perspectives of local communities are represented and taken into account. The use of local languages enables policymakers to engage with community members, understand their needs, and incorporate their input into policy development. When policies are formulated in languages that communities understand and speak fluently, it cultivates a sense of ownership, empowering individuals to contribute to decision-making processes and fostering a sense of collective responsibility for conservation.

Effective Implementation and Compliance

Policies can only achieve their intended outcomes if they are effectively implemented and adhered to by the local communities. Language plays a crucial role in ensuring that policies are implemented correctly. When policies are formulated in local languages, community members can better comprehend the requirements and instructions, facilitating the implementation process. Clear and unambiguous communication in familiar languages helps overcome misunderstandings and ensures that communities can actively participate in the implementation of conservation measures.

Strengthening Community Engagement

Engaging local communities in conservation efforts is essential for long-term success. Language acts as a powerful tool for engaging and involving community members in policy formulation. Public consultations, community meetings, and dialogues conducted in local languages foster open and meaningful communication between policymakers and community members. This engagement builds trust, promotes collaboration, and encourages communities to take ownership of conservation initiatives.

Addressing Cultural Context and Sensitivity

Language carries cultural nuances and expressions that are integral to effective policy formulation. By utilizing local languages, policymakers can capture the cultural context and sensitivity required for conservation policies. Language allows policymakers to frame policies in ways that align with cultural values, beliefs, and practices, ensuring that policies are more likely to be embraced and respected by the local communities.

Overcoming Challenges and Language Barriers

While the use of local languages in policy formulation brings numerous benefits, challenges may arise. Language diversity within the region requires policymakers to navigate the complexities of translation, dialects, and variations in terminology. Adequate resources, skilled translators, and community involvement are crucial in addressing these challenges and ensuring accurate and effective policy communication.

Language plays a pivotal role in policy formulation for effective conservation in the Lake Victoria region. By utilizing local languages, policymakers can enhance accessibility, promote inclusivity, empower communities, and strengthen community engagement. Translating policies into local languages ensures that communities can understand, actively participate in, and implement conservation measures. The use of local languages in policy formulation demonstrates a commitment to community-centered conservation efforts, fostering a sense of shared responsibility for the preservation of natural resources in the Lake Victoria region.

Preserving Traditional Knowledge for Sustainable Resource Management

Traditional knowledge held by indigenous communities is a treasure trove of wisdom accumulated over centuries. In the Lake Victoria region, indigenous languages such as Luo, Luhya, and Kiswahili have served as essential vehicles for the transfer of this traditional knowledge from elders to younger generations. This chapter explores the significant role that language plays in preserving and promoting traditional knowledge, specifically focusing on sustainable resource management practices like farming, fishing, and forestry.

The Value of Indigenous Languages in Knowledge Transmission

Indigenous languages are intimately tied to the cultural and ecological heritage of the Lake Victoria region. They embody the wisdom and experiences of previous generations, including time-tested practices for sustainable resource management. Through the use of indigenous languages, elders pass down knowledge about the natural environment, the behavior of plants and animals, seasonal patterns, and traditional farming techniques. This knowledge forms the foundation for sustainable resource management practices.

Language as a Bridge Between Generations

Language acts as a bridge between generations, ensuring the continuity of traditional knowledge. Indigenous languages enable elders to communicate their wisdom, insights, and practical skills to younger community members. The richness and nuance of these languages allow for precise transmission of knowledge, encompassing not only practical techniques but also cultural values and spiritual connections to the natural world.

Documenting Traditional Knowledge

Language plays a crucial role in the documentation of traditional knowledge. Efforts have been made to collect, record, and preserve indigenous languages, ensuring that traditional knowledge is safeguarded for future generations. These initiatives involve collaborating with community members, linguists, and anthropologists to create comprehensive records, including oral histories, stories, songs, and ecological observations. Documentation in indigenous languages ensures the authenticity and cultural relevance of the recorded knowledge.

Promoting Traditional Knowledge in Education

Integrating traditional knowledge into formal and informal education systems is vital for its preservation and promotion. By utilizing indigenous languages as a medium of instruction, educational programs can incorporate traditional ecological knowledge into the curriculum. This approach strengthens cultural identity, fosters respect for indigenous practices, and equips younger generations with the necessary skills for sustainable resource management.

Applying Traditional Knowledge in Sustainable Resource Management

The application of traditional knowledge in sustainable resource management practices is essential for preserving the ecological balance of the Lake Victoria region. Indigenous languages provide a platform for sharing and disseminating this knowledge, enabling communities to implement sustainable agricultural techniques, adopt responsible fishing practices, and practice forestry in harmony with the ecosystem. By combining traditional wisdom with modern scientific insights, indigenous communities are at the forefront of developing innovative and sustainable approaches to resource management.

Supporting Indigenous Language Revitalization Efforts

Recognizing the importance of indigenous languages in

preserving traditional knowledge, efforts are being made to revitalize and promote these languages. Language revitalization programs include language courses, cultural exchanges, community-led initiatives, and the incorporation of indigenous languages in digital platforms. These efforts not only help to strengthen cultural identity but also contribute to the preservation and promotion of traditional knowledge.

Preserving traditional knowledge is vital for sustainable resource management in the Lake Victoria region. Indigenous languages serve as the vehicle for transmitting this knowledge, connecting generations and safeguarding the wisdom of the past. By documenting and promoting traditional knowledge through indigenous languages, communities can maintain their cultural heritage, strengthen their resilience, and continue to thrive while preserving the rich natural resources of the region. Embracing and supporting indigenous languages is a crucial step toward sustainable development and the conservation of resources in the Lake Victoria region.

Facilitating Community Participation

Local languages have been essential in facilitating community participation in conservation efforts. By using languages that people understand, conservationists can engage the local communities in decision-making processes that directly affect their natural resources. This inclusive approach fosters a sense of ownership and empowers communities to actively contribute to the preservation of their environment.

Monitoring and Evaluation with Language

Language is indispensable in monitoring and evaluating conservation efforts around Lake Victoria. Conservationists can collect valuable feedback and data from the local communities by utilizing local languages. This information serves as a crucial resource for improving future conservation strategies and enhancing the overall effectiveness of resource management.

Conclusion

Language has played a pivotal role in promoting the conservation of resources around the Lake Victoria region by facilitating communication and education among communities. Through the transfer of indigenous knowledge, community engagement, policy development, biodiversity conservation, and cross-cultural communication, language has emerged as a powerful tool for fostering sustainable resource management practices. By recognizing the significance of language and communication, we can continue to harness their potential in the conservation of resources in the Lake Victoria region, ensuring a sustainable and prosperous future for generations to come.

Chapter 13
Conclusion and Recommendations

Conclusion

In this study, we have conducted a broad preliminary investigation into the role of traditional cultural practices in the conservation and management of natural resources in the Lake Victoria region. Our findings have highlighted the significance of cultural practices across various fields and underscored their critical role in conservation efforts. Unfortunately, some of these traditional cultural factors have been lost over time, particularly due to the impact of colonialism. This loss has resulted in a significant decline in biodiversity and soil degradation.

The challenge now lies in reviving the traditional institutions that were once effective in conservation. OSIENALA has been at the forefront of efforts to restore the environmental resources of Lake Victoria. Previously, it was believed that restoration could only be achieved through technological practices imported from foreign countries. However, it is increasingly recognized that traditional methods, which have long been neglected, can play a crucial role in the restoration, rehabilitation, and management of natural resources in the Lake Victoria region.

Recommendations

Based on the fundamental aspects of the lives, regulatory teachings, and practices of the people in the Lake Victoria region revealed by this study, the following recommendations were made during the workshop of elders in Mwanza:

1. **Integration of Traditional Cultural Practices:** It is important to recognize and legitimize the importance of traditional cultural practices, including traditional medicines and cultural values, by integrating them into present management practices.

2. **Empowering Cultural Institutions:** Existing cultural institutions, such as kingdoms, chieftainships, and councils of elders, hold significant potential for conservation and management of natural resources. These institutions should be encouraged, empowered, and facilitated to actively participate in the conservation efforts.

3. **Common Conservation and Management Policies:** Since Lake Victoria is a shared water resource among the three East African countries, there is a need for common conservation and management policies governing its utilization. The East African governments should enforce these policies through the East African Cooperation arrangements.

4. **Formal Institution for Traditional Medicine:** Traditional medicine continues to play a major role in the region, and therefore, a formal institution should be established to coordinate, conserve, and manage the practice of traditional medicine.

5. **Theatrical Plays for Conservation:** Enhancing the conservation of natural resources can be achieved through demonstrations via theatrical plays. A mechanism should be established to transform indigenous stories, songs, proverbs, praises, myths, and legends into dramas enacted by communities and villagers. These plays should focus on applying conservation principles specific to the Lake Victoria region, based on the folklore of each ethnic group.

6. **Annual Rotational Conferences:** Elders from East Africa should organize annual rotational conferences in venues around the lake basin to share progressive cultural practices and consolidate environmental issues. The information gathered should be presented to the East African Assembly, country parliaments, and donor agencies for adoption and implementation.

7. **Lake Victoria Day:** Communities around the lake should initiate an annual Lake Victoria Day dedicated to environmental activities, such as tree planting, beach cleaning, and general education and awareness creation.

8. **Mapping of Cultural Sites:** Urgent comprehensive mapping of cultural sites around Lake Victoria should be conducted to facilitate their conservation, environmental improvement, and tourist attraction. Certain sites, such as Budhangali, should be protected through the East African Community.

By implementing these recommendations, we can harness the power of traditional cultural practices to promote effective conservation and sustainable management of the natural resources in the Lake Victoria region.

Bibliography

1. Amartya Sen, How Does culture Matter? Poverty: Culture and Povert 2001
2. M. Anene Religion and Conservation in Ghana
3. Alexander, J.C. and S. Seidman (Eds) (1990). Culture and Society Londn C.U.P.
4. Ayisi, E.O. (1998). An introduction to the study of African Culture 2nd edition. Nairobi E.A.E.P.
5. Berkes, Fikret, (1998), "Indigenous Knowledge and Resource Management in the Canadian Sub-arctic", in Berkes, Fikret and Carl Folke, (Eds), Linking Socia and Ecological Sysetms: Managemetn Practice and Social mechanisms for Building Resilience, 3 Essays. London: Cambridge University Press.
6. Bangachwa et al (ed) (1994). Poverty Alleviation Recent Research Issues. Dares Salaam University Press.
7. Bantje, H.A (1989) "Review of Literature on Agriculture and Land use in Sukumaland" Working Paper No. 1. Amsterdam Royal Tropical Institute.
8. BArsh, R.L. (1999). "Indigenous Knowledge and Biodiversity" Posey, D.A. (Ed) Culture and Spirital Values of Biodiversity: A Complementary Contribution to the Global Biodiversity Assessment, UNEP, Nairobi.
9. Basil, D. (1967). East and Central African to the Late 19th Century. London Longman.
10. Budelman, A. (1996). "In Search of Sustainability, Nutrients Trees and Farmers Experimentation in North Sukumaland Agriculture". Working Paper No. 16 Amsterdam Royal Tropical Institute.
11. Chapman, Margaret (1987). "Traditional Political Structure and Conservation in Oceania". In Colding Johan and Carl Folke,

The Taboo System: Lessons about Informal Institutions for Nuture Management. 16 Ambio, p. 431.

12. Colding Johan and Carl Folke (2000), "The Taboo System: Lesson about Informal Institutions for Nature Management," The Georgetown International Environmental Law Review, volume XIII, issue 2, p.422.

13. Eriksen, S. et al (1996). Land Tenure and Wildlife Management. Island Press.

14. Falconer, Julia, Non-timber Forest Production in Southern Ghana: Traditional and cultural Forest Values. P.368.

15. FAO (1996). Tanzania Lake Victoria Fisheries Study on Fish Quality Improvement and Related Investment Proposal. FAO: Rome

16. Gerden, C. and Mtallo, "Traditional Forest Reserves in Babati District, Tanzania. A Study in Human Ecology". Working Paper No. 128. Swedish University of Agricultural Science, International Rural Development Centre, 1990. In Bruce John. African Tenure Models at the Turn of the Century: Individual Property Models and common Property Models.

17. Herlocker, D. et al (ed) (1999). Rangeland Resources in East Africa Their iconological and D

18. Lupeja P.M. evelopment Nairobi GTZ.

19. Johannes, Robert. (1978). "Traditional Marine Conservation Methods in Oceania and Their Demise," 9 Annual Review of Ecological Systems. In Colding Johan and Carl Folke, The Taboo System: Lessons about Informal Institution for Nature Management London C.U.P

20. International Centre for Development Oriented Research in Agriculture ((1991), "Analysis of Agriculture and Livestock Production Systems in Misungwi Division" Lake Zone Tanzania, Working Document Series 16.

21. Kamati ya Utafiti was Utamaduni Bujora (1988), Imani za Jadi za Kisukuma Katika Misemo, Hadithi, Methali and Desturi za Maisha. CID.

22. Kapinga R. et al. (1998), "Inventory Cassava Extension Message" Field note 85 Mwanza.

23. Kodasha International. (1994). Japan: Profile of a Nation: Kodasha: Japan.
24. et al (ed) (1996). A collection of Agriculture background information for Mwanza Region. URT, FAO.
25. Madhav Gadgil, Firket Berkes and Carl Folke, Indigenous Knowledge for Biodiversity Conservation Ibidem, p. 154.
26. Malcom D.W. (1953), Sukumaland, An African People and Their Country, A study of Land Use in Tanzanyika London.
27. J.O Malo, 1999: Jaluo: Shadrack Malo. Nairobi, Kenya 74pgs
28. Maloba, Beatrice, The Flooding of River Sio, ibidem, p.415.
29. Mboya, P. Luo Kitgi Gi Timbegi Kisumu, Anyange Press (1983)
30. Moles, Jerry and Senanayake, Ranil, Voices of the Earth, ibidem, p. 149.
31. Msambichaka, L.A, et al (ed) Development challenge and strategies for Tanzania Dares Salaam University Press.
32. Natiziger E. Wayne, (1996), The Economics of Developing Countries.
33. Ngazi H. et al (ed) (February 2000), A Study of Indigenous Knowledge of Soil nad Water Mahjiga Village, Sukumaland . European Commission
34. Ng'weno, Fleur, Seasonal Wetlands, ibidem, p. 414.
35. Niamir, Maryam, Traditional Woodland Management Techniques of African Pastoralists, Unasylva, V. 41 (160), 1990, p 50.
36. Ntiamoa-Baidu, Conservation of Costal Lagoons in Ghana: The Traditional Approach, 20 Landscape and Rban Planning, 1991, cited in the Colding Johan nad Folke Carl, The Taboo System: Lessons about Informal Institutions for Nature Management, Ibidem, P. 431.
37. Ogot, B.A. et al (ed) Zamani: A survey of East African History Nairobi EAPH and Longman (1968).
38. Ogot, G. The promised land Nairobi EAPE (1966)
39. Ogutu, B.O. Keep my Words Nairobi Heinnemann Kenya (1974)
40. Ong'ang'a, O. Lake Victoria / Baltic Sea Seminar on sustainable Development in Lake Victoria and The Baltic Sea Stocklm Sweden (Aug. 2001) unpublished.

41. Osseweijer, Manon, Competition between ancestors and Chinese traders in he Aru islands, Indonesia, ibidem, p. 417.

42. Parajuli, Pramod, Peasant Cosmovisions and Biodiversity; Some Reflections from South Asia, ibidem, p. 387.

43. Per Assmo et ali. (ed)) (1999), Soil Conservation in Arusha Region Tanzania. RELMA (Land Management Unit).

44. Research institutions in Kenya, Tanzania, Uganda and the Netherlands (April 1993), Conservation of Biodiversity and Promotion of Sustainable Development in the Lake Victoria Basin. Netherlands.

45. Roland Oliver et ali. (ed) (1971), A History of East Africa, Volume One. Oxford.

46. Rounce N.V. (1946), The Agriculture of te Cultivation Steppe of the Lake, Wesern and Central Provinces, Longman, Green and Co. Cape Town.

47. Ruddle, K. andZhong G. Integrate Agriculture – Aquaculture in South China London CUP (1988).

48. Soemardjan, S. and K.W. Thomson Culture, Development and Democracy: The role of the interllectual United Nations University Press Japan (1994.

49. Steiner, William, The Loss of Cultural Diversity and marine Resources sustainability The Impact in Hawaii, ibidem. P. 488-419

50. United Republic of Tanzania (1994), Environmental Statistics Tanzania

51. United Republic of Tanzania (1998), Inventory of Closed Fishing Areas in Emin Pasha Gulf. Tanzania and Mara Shirati Bay Tanzania

52. Blench, R., & Walsh, M. T. (2009). The ecology of language in the Lake Victoria basin. In Language and ecology: Proceedings of the symposium on language and ecology (pp. 1-16).

53. Fisher, B., & Christopher, T. (2007). Poverty and biodiversity: measuring the overlap of human poverty and the biodiversity hotspots. Ecological Economics, 62(1), 93-101.

54. Githeko, A. K., Lindsay, S. W., Confalonieri, U. E., & Patz, J. A. (2000). Climate change and vector-borne diseases: a regional

analysis. Bulletin of the World Health Organization, 78(9), 1136-1147.

55. Hountondji, P. J.

56. Okech, R. N. (2019). Language, knowledge and resource management: The role of indigenous language in promoting sustainable development in Africa. Journal of Sustainable Development in Africa, 21(2), 146-162.

57. Mwaura, P., & Mucai, R. (2016). The role of local languages in natural resource management: The case of Lake Victoria Basin in Kenya. Journal of African Studies and Development, 8(3), 33-41.

58. Leisher, C., Kremen, C., & Ricketts, T. (2011). Using indigenous and scientific knowledge to inform management of freshwater ecosystems in the Lake Victoria Basin. Journal of Environmental Management, 92(2), 331-339.

59. Ondicho, J., & Wagah, G. (2017). Role of local languages in promoting environmental conservation and sustainable development: A case study of Kenya. Journal of Language, Technology & Entrepreneurship in Africa, 8(1), 1-15.

60. Kaburu, H., & Nyangito, M. (2015). The role of indigenous knowledge in conservation of biodiversity in Lake Victoria Basin. Journal of Agriculture and Environmental Sciences, 4(2), 36-45.

www.ingramcontent.com/pod-product-compliance
Lightning Source LLC
Chambersburg PA
CBHW070344270326
41926CB00017B/3982